WATCHABLE BIRDS
of the BLACK HILLS, BADLANDS,
and NORTHERN GREAT PLAINS

Jan L. Wassink

Mountain Press Publishing Company
Missoula, Montana
2006

All photos by the author except as noted

Front cover photograph: Black-billed Magpie
Back cover photograph: Sandhill Crane courtship display
Background cover photo: North Dakota landscape

Library of Congress Cataloging-in-Publication Data

Wassink, Jan L.
  Watchable birds of the Black Hills, Badlands, and northern Great Plains / Jan
L. Wassink.
      p. cm.
  Includes bibliographical references and index.
  ISBN 0-87842-526-8 (pbk. : alk. paper)
  1. Birds—Great Plains—Identification. 2. Birds—Great Plains—Pictorial
works. 3. Bird watching—Great Plains—Guidebooks.   I. Title.
QL683.G68W37 2006
598.07'23478—dc22

                    2006022086

PRINTED IN HONG KONG BY MANTEC PRODUCTION COMPANY

Mountain Press Publishing Company
P.O. Box 2399
Missoula, Montana 59806
(406) 728-1900

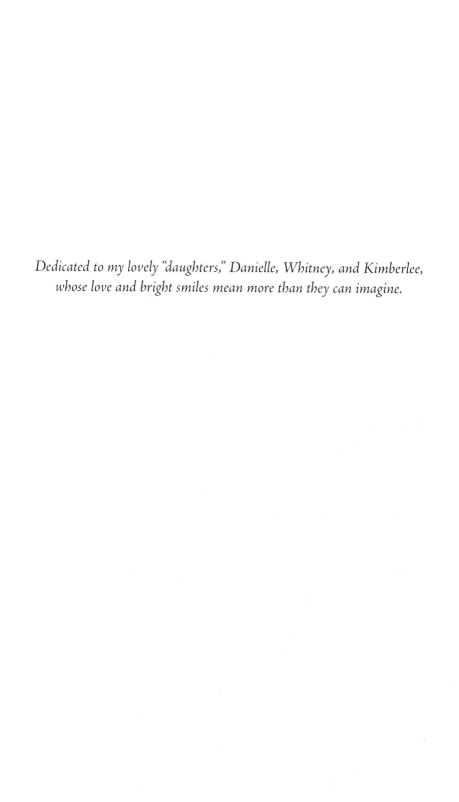

Dedicated to my lovely "daughters," Danielle, Whitney, and Kimberlee, whose love and bright smiles mean more than they can imagine.

Male Mountain Bluebird

TABLE OF CONTENTS

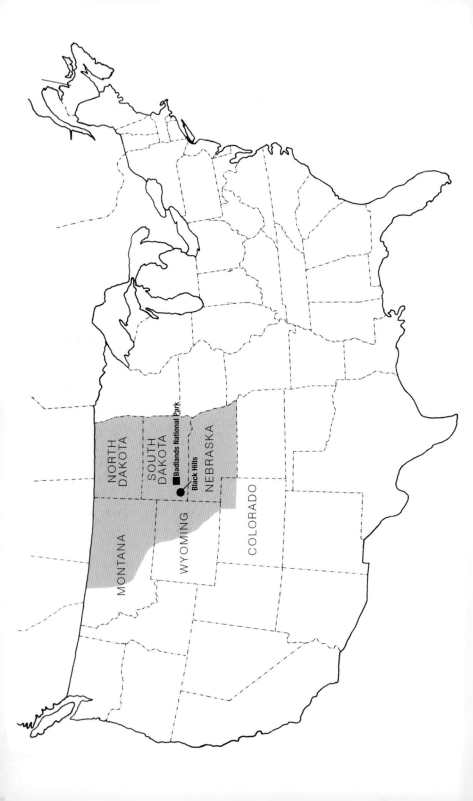

NORTH DAKOTA

SOUTH DAKOTA

Badlands National Park

Black Hills

NEBRASKA

MONTANA

WYOMING

COLORADO

THE BLACK HILLS, BADLANDS, AND SURROUNDING PLAINS

With its diverse range of habitats and central location, this area is home to a remarkable variety of bird species, and offers a bonanza for birdwatchers. In this region, birders can observe some of the boreal species of the north in close proximity to plains species from further south. Likewise, some birds of the eastern deciduous forests share habitats with Rocky Mountain species from the west.

This book covers the Northern Great Plains as defined by the U.S.–Canadian border to the north; the eastern borders of North Dakota, South Dakota, and Nebraska to the east; to the south by the southern border of Nebraska and an extension of that border west to Denver, CO; and to the west by the eastern foothills of the Rocky Mountains, which roughly connect Denver, CO; Cheyenne, Casper, and Buffalo, WY; and Billings, Great Falls, and Shelby, MT. Within those boundaries is included all of the states of North Dakota, South Dakota (including the Black Hills and Badlands National Park), and Nebraska; the northeast corner of Colorado; and the eastern parts of Montana and Wyoming.

The topography of the area varies greatly from the relatively high, dry plains adjacent to the foothills of the Rocky Mountains on the west to the low, moist Missouri River bottoms in extreme southeast Nebraska. In between, this inclined plain is dotted with upthrust formations that form a myriad of buttes and relatively small, isolated mountain ranges. The plain has been cut into insular plateaus through erosion by the Missouri River system, the dominant system in the region. The Missouri River and its tributaries drain the majority of the region. The James River in North Dakota and the Platte River in Nebraska are the other two large river systems in the region. Other topographical features include areas of sand dunes and extensive areas of badland habitats.

Elevations in the region range from a high of 7,242 feet on Harney Peak in the Black Hills to a low of 850 feet on the Missouri River in the southeastern corner of Nebraska.

Precipitation varies from a high of 32 inches per year in southeast Nebraska to a low of about 15 inches per year in most of eastern Montana. Differing precipitation rates, coupled with the varied topography and soil types, result in a wide variety of vegetation types as well. Historic habitats, beginning in

1

the east, were dominated by grasslands and transitioned from tallgrass prairie habitats in the east, to short-grass prairie further west, and finally to bunch-grass habitats in the foothills of the far west. The species include bluestem grasses in the eastern tall-grass; mixed bluestem and wheatgrass-needlegrass in the transition prairies; grama-buffalo grass in the short-grass prairies; and bunchgrass in the far west. In addition, the Nebraska Sandhills prairie is its own unique habitat. Finally, these grassland habitats and the sagebrush lands and mixed brushlands in the west merge into coniferous forests on the higher elevations of the Black Hills of South Dakota and elsewhere in the region; into the badland habitats of Teddy Roosevelt National Park in North Dakota and Badlands National Park in South Dakota; and into a variety of deciduous forests in the river bottoms and lowlands.

Unfortunately, only small remnants of these natural grasslands remain in the region, and birds that relied on these historic habitats—such as the Greater Prairie-Chicken—have declined along with the loss of these habitats. Agriculture and urban expansion have replaced the historic prairie grasslands, and now provide habitats for bird species that are able to exploit these conditions, like the Ring-necked Pheasant and European Starling.

The Northern Great Plains: North Dakota

INTRODUCTION

Approximately forty million people in North America classify themselves as birdwatchers, and more are becoming interested every day. This book is primarily intended for those who are relatively new to birding and are beginning to be interested in questions beyond simple identification. This book will help you learn to identify the birds included, but it also highlights some of their behaviors—how they hunt or gather food, which habitats they use and, when possible, which of their characteristics make them able to live and thrive in that particular habitat. It also helps you know where and when to look for a particular species in this region.

Organization of This Book

Birding checklists of this region contain well over 400 of the more than 800 species found in North America. These checklists include those of the national parks, national monuments, national recreation areas, and national wildlife refuges, as well as the checklists from the many state parks, state recreation areas, and wildlife management areas in the region.

Of the more than 400 species seen in this region, I have chosen to highlight 77 species that I believe are some of the most interesting and most likely to be seen by beginning birders. I have tried to include enough information in the natural history section to make this a companion volume to some of the more basic field guides to the birds of this area.

In addition to the descriptions of the 82 birds I have chosen to highlight, I have included photos of 71 additional species that might also be seen in this area. For example, I have chosen to write a detailed species account of the Western Grebe. I have also included a photo of the very similar Clark's Grebe and a few notes on how the Clark's Grebe differs from the Western Grebe. When the male and female of a species are dimorphic (differing in appearance), I have tried to include photos of both sexes.

I have also included the six endangered species that migrate through or breed in this region because I believe you have a reasonable chance to see them at some time. They are the Trumpeter Swan, Whooping Crane, Bald Eagle, Peregrine Falcon, Least Tern, and Piping Plover. These species have been seriously affected by human changes to the environment; while the Trumpeter Swan, Whooping Crane, Bald Eagle, and Peregrine Falcon are responding well to conservation efforts, there are many challenges ahead to make the changes necessary to positively affect the Least Tern and Piping Plover populations.

Scientific Names

The nomenclature in this book follows *The A.O.U. Check-list of North American Birds*, Seventh Edition, published by the American Ornithologists' Union, including the capitalization of the AOU common names. I generally follow the AOU species order, with one exception: many of the "similar species" appear with the species account of the bird they may be mistaken for, rather than in their generally accepted order.

I have listed only the accepted common name of the species and also its currently accepted Latin name. Scientists classify all living organisms according to their physical similarities and differences. The seven divisions in this classification system are—from the most general to the most specific— kingdom, phylum, class, order, family, genus, and species. All birds belong to the Kingdom Animalia, Phylum Chordata, Subphylum Vertebrata, and Class Aves.

Progressing further, the American Robin, for example, belongs to the Order Passeriformes (perching birds) and the Family Turdidae (thrushes). The table of contents of this book is grouped by order and family, and these names are given in the introduction to each section of species accounts to show the relationships of the birds in that section.

The Latin name given in the species description includes the genus and species name, i.e., *Turdus migratorious*. The first word of the Latin name is the genus name, *Turdus*. A genus includes one or more similar species that do not normally interbreed with each other. The species name, *migratorious*, is

Partial albino American Robin

Snowy Egret

the second word and is given to a group of individual birds that exhibit very similar characteristics and breed with each other when given the opportunity. Taken together, the two names form a unique scientific name, so a scientist anywhere in the world reading about *Turdus migratorious* knows that he is reading about the American Robin and not the robin found in Europe.

How to Use This Book

You have just seen a predominantly black-and-white bird with a long tail fly across the road just west of the Black Hills. How do you find that bird in this book? First of all, to avoid looking at every photo in the book each time you see an unfamiliar bird, it helps to become familiar with the general size and shape of different types of birds and where they are located in this book. For example, you probably already know the black-and-white bird you saw is not a duck or goose, not a hawk or eagle, not a hummingbird or sparrow, and so on. So, you can look through the table of contents and go to the illustrations of some of the groups of birds that offer the best possibilities. Eventually, following this method, you will end up in the "jay" section and discover that the common name of the unfamiliar bird is "Black-billed Magpie." With practice, you will soon be able to turn almost immediately to the correct section to locate an unknown species.

Eventually you will see a bird that is not included in this book. For those species, you will need to consult a more complete field guide (see the Suggested References). However, by reading the description of the various families of birds, you should be able to conclude that the robin-sized bird with an extremely thick bill is very similar to the grosbeaks included in this book. A brief glance at the grosbeaks in a field guide should lead you to the correct species of grosbeak very quickly.

Male American Goldfinch

To speed this process, it helps to look at the next group up the scientific classification system: the family. A family includes one or more genera, or genuses. For example, the area covered by this book includes eight species of the swallow family (Family Hirundinidae) from four different genera. The family name of each of the birds is given in the introduction to that section. Likewise, groups of similar families make up an order. The swallows belong to a larger group called the perching birds (Order Passeriformes). If you can learn the general characteristics of each of the orders of birds, you will be able to narrow down your search for the identification of a new bird much more quickly.

In the species account for each bird, the **"Field marks"** section describes characteristics of the bird that you will probably be able to see in the field. The size, an important factor in identifying birds, leads the list. The measurements, in inches, indicate the length from the tip of the bill to the tip of the tail as seen in the wild. While you may never be able to accurately guess the length of a wild bird, for identification purposes, being able to recognize that a new bird looks slightly larger or slightly smaller than a species you are already familiar with, (e.g., American Robin) will give you a helpful guide to its actual size. While many species may resemble each other superficially, each species has a unique combination of characteristics that distinguish it. Those identifying characteristics are highlighted in **bold type.** The rest of the field marks section outlines general characteristics of the bird. The "Duck Wing" and "Parts of a Bird" diagrams on p. 212 identify terms used in this section.

The **"Status"** section describes the distribution of the bird in this region, its relative abundance, the seasons to look for it there, and the bird's breeding status in the region. "The region" or "this area" refers to the entire area covered by the book (see map on p. viii).

I have used the following abbreviations:

BH: Black Hills

BLNP: Badlands National Park

NG: National Grassland

NM: National Monument

NWR: National Wildlife Refuge

SP: State Park

SRA: State Recreation Area

SWA: State Wildlife Area

WMA: Wildlife Management Area

WMD: Wildlife Management District

WPA: Waterfowl Production Area

STATE NAMES

CO: Colorado

MT: Montana

ND: North Dakota

NE: Nebraska

SD: South Dakota

WY: Wyoming

A *resident* bird lives in the region year-round, while a *summer resident* is present only in spring and summer. A *breeder* nests and raises young within the region. *Winter visitors* frequent the region between mid-December and late February, while *migrants* travel through the area on their annual spring and/or fall migrations.

Relative abundance, in decreasing order, is listed as *abundant, common, fairly common, uncommon, rare, occasional*, and *accidental*.

The **"Hot spots"** section shows places where you may have an especially good chance of observing a species. I have included this section only for species that are relatively rare, but where there is a good chance of seeing them at a particular place, and also for species that occur in very large numbers at certain times of year. I did not include hot spots for species that are very widespread, or for species that are so rare that there is no dependable place to see them.

Mallards grunt-whistling

Before visiting these hot spots, it would be wise to contact the governing agency for that area and plan your visit with their help. The "Birding Destinations" section on pp. 220–25 highlights some sites that are worthy of a special effort to visit. You can also check the "Suggested References" section for books that include tips on when and where to see particular birds.

The main description in the species account covers each bird's natural history. This includes the bird's niche—how, when, and where it feeds, builds its nest, attracts mates, and, where applicable, whether its populations are increasing or decreasing. Look in the main description for distinctive behaviors that can aid in identification. Keep in mind that many of these behaviors are common to the entire family, so information may not be repeated in subsequent species accounts.

The calls or songs of most species are diagnostic once you know them. However, written descriptions of songs proved of very little use to me when I started watching birds. I have only included written descriptions of songs and calls that are simple and distinctive. When you reach the point where you want to learn to bird by sound, check the "Suggested References" section for the latest guides to bird songs.

Observing Birds

The best place to watch birds is wherever you are at the moment. While that may sound flippant, I have actually enjoyed many more hours of watching birds while I was engaged in other activities than I have by specifically setting aside time to go birding. I suspect many people with an interest in birds are like me and will catch moments of birding pleasure while doing other things.

When you have time to devote exclusively to birding, you probably do not need to venture further than a nearby city park, lakeshore, or river bottom. By finding a good place to bird close to home, you can familiarize yourself with that area and the birds that frequent it—where their territories are, where they feed, where they nest, and how they behave.

Still, birding in new territory, looking for new species, and watching huge concentrations of birds in staging areas or on breeding grounds are too exciting to overlook. I had originally intended to have a section in this book on where to go in this region to see these spectacular sights. For example, according to the American Bird Conservancy, more than 20 of the "500 Most Important Bird Areas" in the U.S. are in this region. However, I soon came to realize that describing the myriad of great places to watch birds in this region would fill a book all by itself. So, while I have included a list of "Birding Destinations" instead, I recommend you begin by talking to local birders or checking with your state wildlife officials. In addition, check out the nearest national wildlife refuge. The personnel there will most likely be more than happy to suggest places to visit to satisfy your increasing interest in birds.

A relatively new development in birding is the concept of birding trails. Both North Dakota and South Dakota have recently published guides to birding trails with automobile routes that go through excellent birding habitat. The guides usually also list the best times to go and a list of species you might encounter. Montana is currently working on such a guide, and by the

Male and Female Mallards tipping

time this goes to press, some of the other states may have published something similar. Check the Internet for the latest information.

If you are looking for a particular bird, you will greatly increase your success and enjoyment if you look when they are most active. For example, if you want to see owls, most of them are most easily located by going out at night and listening for their territorial hooting. However, if you are trying to locate a diurnal owl such as the Burrowing Owl, obviously you will have the most success during the day. Likewise, many waterfowl are common during the spring and fall migrations, but do not breed or winter here. If you want to see Sharp-tailed Grouse and Greater Prairie-Chickens displaying, you will need to go in April or May. For huge concentrations of Sandhill Cranes along the Platte River in Nebraska or giant flocks of Snow Geese at some of the national wildlife refuges, you will need to go look for them in the spring when they are passing through. Again, if you know what you want to see, contact the personnel in that area to find out the best time to visit.

The Ethics of Birding

Finding food, defending territories, raising young, migrating, escaping predators, and seeking shelter from the weather require a tremendous amount of energy and make life tenuous at best for birds. In our desire to see them and learn more about them, we need to use common sense to avoid disrupting their lives and destroying the very thing we seek to enjoy.

In general, small birds tolerate more human disturbance than larger species. Still, birds are individuals, and each one may have a different level of tolerance for humans. I have photographed small birds from a few feet away without the aid of a blind while the birds went about their business with no indication that they even noticed I was around. On the other hand, with some raptors, simply stopping a vehicle a quarter of a mile away will prompt them to take flight. In some cases, one bird of a pair will be much more tolerant of human presence than the other bird.

Disturbances near active nests may result in failure of the nest and the loss of the production from that breeding pair for the entire year. Agitation, repeated alarm calls, aggressive behavior, or distraction displays are all signs that you may be too close to a nest or young and you should back off. With some species, you may have to leave the area entirely before the birds will settle down.

Most birds are particularly sensitive to disturbances early in the nesting cycle, and even inadvertent disturbances in the area during the nest-building or egg-laying stage may result in the pair abandoning the nest. As incubation proceeds, the female becomes increasingly bonded to the nest and thus less likely to abandon it. As fledging approaches, the adults are unlikely to abandon the nest, but other possibilities crop up with too much disturbance.

A photographer keeps a respectful distance from a nesting box.

Until hatchlings develop feathers, they are incapable of regulating their own body temperature, and the adults must brood the young to keep them warm. If your presence keeps the adults away from the nest too long, exposure to even moderate temperatures may greatly weaken the young. In some cases, they will die—without giving you any indication that something was amiss. In addition, too much activity around a nest may flatten the grass or otherwise expose the nest to increased predation by attracting attention to the nest site through scent or by exposing it to view.

Birding is most enjoyable and most educational when you can observe the birds going about their normal activities. Around their nest is not the only place we may cause undue stress to birds. Repeatedly flushing birds from their favored feeding areas can eventually force them to remain in areas with less food, depriving them of needed energy. Whenever you are around birds, be conscious of the pressure you are putting on them and minimize it as much as possible.

Birding is an enjoyable activity and, with care, we can participate in it without harming the birds in any way. For more reading on this topic, see the "Code of Birding Ethics" available on the American Birding Association Web site.

Welcome to the wonderful world of birding.

GEESE, SWANS, AND DUCKS
ORDER ANSERIFORMES

Waterfowl (Family Anatidae) are, not surprisingly, well suited to spending most of their lives on water. Their flat bodies increase buoyancy and their fluffy down insulation wards off the chill of cold water. Long necks allow them to reach deep into the water to feed, and their flattened bills, equipped with toothlike edges called lamellae, enable them to strain tiny food items from the water. Short, powerful legs and webs between the three front toes propel them through the water. When northern lakes begin to freeze, their narrow, pointed wings carry them to warmer climes far to the south. The young are covered with down and leave the nest soon after hatching.

Canada Goose with solar radio collar

Geese are intermediate in size, weight, and neck length between the swans and the ducks. Like swans, the sexes are similar, they mate for life, and they share domestic responsibilities. With legs set farther forward on their bodies than swans and ducks, geese are more mobile on land and do more grazing and feeding on waste grain.

Trumpeter Swan

Swans, with their pure white plumage, large size, and long necks, are by far the most visually impressive of the waterfowl. Swans feed on submerged plants by dipping their head and neck in shallow water. Birds living in areas with high concentrations of dissolved iron in the water often have rust stains on their heads and upper necks. The male (cob) and the female (pen) mate for life and usually raise two young (cygnets) each year.

Perching ducks frequent wooded swamps, ponds, and marshes. They are relatively short legged and long tailed, are often brightly colored, and have claws that aid them in perching on branches, which other ducks rarely do.

Dabbling ducks, like swans and geese, feed from the surface of the water by tipping. Limited by their smaller size and shorter necks, they cannot reach as far into the water as the large birds and consequently frequent

Dabbling duck:
Northern Pintail

shallow water. Unlike the larger waterfowl, ducks are dimorphic, with the male being the larger and more colorful of the pair and the female appearing nondescript. Both sexes sport a bright patch of color, called a speculum, on the secondary flight feathers on their wings. Instead of requiring a running start like the rest of the waterfowl, dabbling ducks leap vertically into the air from the surface of the water. They nest on land. Primarily vegetarians, they also eat a variety of small invertebrates and fish during the nesting season.

Diving duck:
Common Goldeneye

Diving ducks prefer the open water of fairly large, deep rivers, lakes, and reservoirs, and feed by diving, as their name suggests. They winter mostly along the coastal bays on both coasts and the Gulf of Mexico, moving to inland marshes in spring to nest. Unlike surface ducks, which nest on land, most divers build their nests over water. Diving ducks take flight by running across the surface of the water until they gain enough momentum to become airborne. Their larger feet, lobed hind toe, and legs set farther back on their bodies make them more powerful swimmers than the surface ducks but more awkward on land.

Stiff-tailed ducks are small, compact ducks with long, spiky tails that they often hold upright. They inhabit open ponds and bays.

Mergansers have long, slender bills with toothlike serrations along the edges that allow them to grasp fish.

Common Merganser

GEESE

Snow Goose
Chen caerulescens

FIELD MARKS: 29 inches. Small; **all-white plumage; rosy pink bill with a black grin patch**; black wing tips; there is also a blue morph with a dark gray body.

STATUS: Abundant migrant in the eastern part of the region; not found in the BH.

HOT SPOTS: DeSoto NWR, NE; Sand Lake NWR, SD; Des Lacs NWR, ND.

The noisiest of the geese, Snow Geese gather on large marshes and grain fields, where the din of their calling can be heard at great distances. The spring migration can be spectacular in this region, with upwards of a million birds sometimes congregating at Sand Lake National Wildlife Refuge in South Dakota.

Originally thought to be two separate species, the Snow Goose and Blue Goose are now classified as two color morphs of a single species. The midcontinental population of the white phase winters along the Gulf Coast and migrates along the Central and Eastern flyways, which pass through the eastern part of this region. The bulk of the population of the blue phase also winters along the Gulf Coast and migrates through this area in the spring and fall.

Over the last thirty years, various factors have provided almost ideal circumstances for Snow Geese, and populations have exploded. On their wintering grounds along the Gulf Coast, where the birds once fed on tubers of slough grass, they are now feeding in rice fields. On their way north they once encountered mile upon mile of plowed fields; with the adoption of minimum-till farming practices by grain farmers, the geese now feed on waste grain in crop stubble fields. Over the course of their two- or three-month northerly migration these geese may have gained as much as two pounds, and reach their breeding grounds in top condition.

Biologists are concerned because the midcontinental population of "light" geese (including Snow Geese and Ross's Geese) has grown from approximately 1.3 million birds in 1973 to about 3.9 million birds in 1997. It has gotten to the point where the breeding grounds are being destroyed by overgrazing. The hungry adults arrive in the Arctic before green-up, grubbing down into the mud in search of stems and roots, consequently destroying the plants before they even begin to grow. Those plants that escape discovery and actually sprout are often pulled up by the roots. Plants that survive into summer are weakened by the constant cropping. As the vegetation disappears, more and more mudflats are exposed to the sun and evaporation increases, pulling water to the surface from deeper in the subsoil. As that water evaporates, the salt that was dissolved in the water crystallizes on the surface, effectively poisoning the soil so even less vegetation grows the following year. As this process continues, the geese move further and further into previously unused areas, destroying the vegetation as they go.

In response fall bag limits and hunting season lengths were increased from 1990 until 1995, when they reached the limits allowed by the Migratory Bird Treaty Act. Populations were still growing, so spring hunts were instituted in the United States and Canada in 1999. Biologists believe that approximately 1.4 million light geese will need to be harvested each year to control these populations and prevent more permanent damage to breeding grounds.

Snow Goose. —Photo by Tom J. Ulrich
Inset: *Snow Goose (blue morph)*

Snow Geese

Canada Goose *Branta canadensis*

FIELD MARKS: 36 inches. **Black head and neck; white cheek patch;** brownish back and sides.

STATUS: Common resident breeder throughout the area, including the BH and BLNP.

HOT SPOTS: Crosby WMD and Lake Zahl NWR, Crosby, ND; Lacreek NWR, SD.

The wedge-shaped skeins of "honkers," or Canada Geese, that grace the autumn skies are known across the country as a sure sign of fall. Canada Geese are extremely adaptable birds and are the best-known and most widely distributed goose in North America. Depending on the source, there are between six and twelve subspecies of Canada Geese, ranging in size from the diminutive 25-inch, 3-pound Cackling Goose (*B.c. hutchinsii*) of the Pacific Coast to the 45-inch, 9-pound Giant Canada Goose (*B. c. maxima*) that is native to this region. Nearly eliminated by the early 1900s, Canada Geese populations have recovered as the result of conservation and reintroduction efforts. By 2004, there were in excess of 100,000 *B. c. maxima* individuals in South Dakota alone; the management goal is to sustain this population level in the future.

Several subspecies pass through this region during migration, with the Giant Canada Goose arriving in early March and the others piling in around the end of March. Those that stay in the region to nest set up territories in larger wetlands and shallow lakes with emergent vegetation. Their ability to nest anywhere they can find a site relatively protected from predators—on cliffs, in Osprey nests, on small islands, atop muskrat mounds, and in a variety of human-made nest structures—has made it possible for biologists to introduce breeding populations to many new areas. In fact, Canada Geese have been so successful at colonizing new areas that they have become a nuisance in many city parks, subdivisions, and golf course ponds.

The territorial and mating displays of Canada Geese are varied and interesting. *Bent-neck, head-forward, head-pumping, upright-neck, head-down, head-flip, rolling, neck-dipping, head-up,* and a wide variety of calls all have specific meaning to other geese and to informed observers. Territorial defense disappears as soon as the young hatch and the family concerns itself with foraging.

After the young have learned to fly, the family groups join together and form large flocks. These flocks spend their days feeding in nearby fields and their nights resting on large rivers, lakes, and reservoirs. During mild winters, many Canada Geese spend the winter in the region, roosting on open water and making noisy flights to feeding areas. If winter weather eliminates the open water or heavy snow cover makes foraging difficult, the flocks move further south until they find the necessary open water and available food.

Canada Geese

Canada Goose with goslings

SWANS

Trumpeter Swan *Cygnus buccinator*

FIELD MARKS: 65 inches. Large; white plumage; black bill; **best distinguished from the Tundra Swan by its resonant call.**

STATUS: Endangered species. Reintroduced species and local breeder; rare in BH and BLNP.

HOT SPOTS: Lacreek NWR, SD; Valentine NWR and Crescent Lake NWR, NE.

Between 1853 and 1877, Hudson's Bay Company handled more than 17,000 swan skins, a good portion of them Trumpeters. The company sold these skins in London for adornments and for use in powder puffs and down garments. Extensive hunting continued until 1933, when only sixty-nine Trumpeter Swans were known to exist in the lower forty-eight states—all in the Yellowstone area. The establishment in 1935 of Red Rock Lakes National Wildlife Refuge in Montana, with its abundance of shallow, slow-moving water of the type preferred by the Trumpeter, protected the breeding habitat of these magnificent birds. The population slowly increased until the 1950s, when it reached about 600 birds. Since then, transplants to other areas in the lower forty-eight states, including some in the 1960s to Lacreek National Wildlife Refuge in Bennett County, South Dakota, have helped reestablish breeding populations. Trumpeter Swans are now regular breeders in and around Lacreek.

——SIMILAR SPECIES——

Tundra Swan *Cygnus columbianus*

FIELD MARKS: 53 inches. Large; white plumage; black bill, often with a **yellow spot in front of the eye.** Distinguished from Trumpeter Swan by its voice, **a high-pitched yelp.**

STATUS: Common migrant throughout the region except the BH and BLNP.

HOT SPOTS: Des Lacs NWR, ND; Barnes Lake WPA, Woodworth, ND.

Among the earliest spring migrants, large flocks of Tundra Swans leave their favored winter feeding areas along the Gulf Coast of Texas and head north to breed on the Arctic tundra. Their narrow, pointed, powerful wings make a whistling sound during flight. The birds were formerly called Whistling Swans because of this sound; they have recently been renamed to reflect the area in which they breed.

Trumpeter Swan

Tundra Swans

PERCHING DUCKS

Wood Duck
Aix sponsa

FIELD MARKS: 13 inches. *Male:* red eye and bill; green head with striped crest; burgundy chest; white belly; buff sides; long tail. *Female:* gray head and crest; white eye patch; brownish gray sides; white belly.

STATUS: Common migrant throughout the eastern part of the region and summer resident along the wooded rivers and streams in eastern Nebraska and the Dakotas; less common but increasing in Montana and Wyoming.

HOT SPOTS: Wood Duck WMA, Stanton, NE.

Named for their affinity for the calm waters of swamps, ponds, lakes, and backwaters surrounded by trees, wood ducks are the most colorful of the ducks. Iridescent colors cover the drake from head to tail. Flights through the woods surrounding their home waters are surprisingly rapid, with the birds navigating nimbly between the trees.

As settlers advanced through the eastern hardwood forests, clearing the land as they went, fewer and fewer tree cavities remained for the Wood Ducks, and they were almost extinct by the early 1900s. Hunting restrictions and other preservation efforts met with some success, and nest-box programs were a key factor in the recovery of this species.

After a prolonged period of courtship displays that may last from late fall and on through the winter, a pair-bond is established and the pair begins their search for an appropriate nest hole. The tree itself is usually near water and in an open cluster of trees rather than solitary or in a dense cluster.

The females usually lay about fourteen eggs in their own nest, but Wood Duck females often "dump" eggs in the nests of other females. Before incubation begins with the laying of the last egg, the nest may contain as many as twenty eggs – five or six of which have been laid by clandestine females. The matriarch of the nest incubates all the eggs and raises the young as though they were all her own. The male does not assist the female with incubation. By the time the eggs hatch at about twenty-four days, he has abandoned her and wandered off to join other males for his summer molt.

Because incubation starts after the last egg is laid, the young hatch within hours of each other. Shortly after hatching, the young scramble to the opening and fearlessly launch themselves into the air. After plummeting as much as 30 feet to the ground, they bounce unhurt off the forest litter and gravitate toward the calling of the mother and the other ducklings, and the entire entourage heads to nearby shallows to feed.

Meanwhile, the males are going through a molt and grow eclipse plumage, the duller, nondescript plumage they keep for a couple of months before molting again into their bright breeding plumage. The dull plumage during this period presumably makes them less visible to predators while they shed both their flight feathers and their tail feathers and are temporarily flightless.

Male Wood Duck

Pair of Wood Ducks

SURFACE DUCKS

Mallard
Anas platyrhynchos

FIELD MARKS: 16 inches. *Male:* **green head;** white neck ring; chestnut breast; blue speculum. *Female:* mottled brown plumage; **yellowish bill;** blue speculum; whitish tail.

STATUS: Abundant permanent resident throughout the area, including the BH and BLNP.

The most abundant and familiar duck in this region and on the continent, the Mallard is the ancestor of most domestic ducks. Highly adaptable, Mallards make themselves at home wherever they find suitable shallow water. Like the rest of the surface ducks (or dabbling ducks), Mallards usually feed from the surface of the water by tipping. Occasionally, they may make shallow dives to reach tidbits in slightly deeper water. When waste grain is available nearby, Mallards may leave the safety of the water and venture into wet fields to forage. These hardy birds can endure fierce cold, needing only open water and food to survive. Where some degree of protection accompanies suitable habitat, such as in city parks and other preserves, populations can expand to the point of becoming a problem.

Pair-bonds are established beginning in late fall and through the winter. Mallards use a wide variety of displays in courtship and bonding. *Head-shakes, tail-shakes, grunt-whistles, down-up, head-up-tail-up, nod-swimming,* and *pumping* can all be observed throughout the winter, although these displays become more frequent as spring approaches. Once the pair-bond is formed, the two birds begin reconnaissance flights over suitable habitat, usually grasslands, to select a nest site. Once the site is selected, the pair builds a nest, and the female begins laying her eggs. As incubation proceeds, the pair-bond begins to dissolve; eventually the drake moves to a nearby marsh where he joins other males and undergoes his annual molt.

——SIMILAR SPECIES——

Gadwall
Anas strepera

FIELD MARKS: 20 inches. *Male:* **gray plumage; black rump;** white speculum. *Female:* mottled brown plumage; unspotted orange bill; white speculum.

STATUS: Fairly common migrant throughout the area, including the BH and BLNP; common breeder in the east.

Easily mistaken for the rather nondescript brown females of other duck species, Gadwalls are often overlooked. More prone to dive than the other dabbling ducks, they seem to prefer stagnant sloughs where they feed on aquatic vegetation. They are also excellent walkers and often feed in woodlands and grain fields.

Male Mallard

Female Mallard

Male Gadwall

Blue-winged Teal
Anas discors

FIELD MARKS: 15 inches. *Male:* small; slate gray head; **white crescent in front of eye;** green speculum; pale blue upper wing coverts. *Female:* brown plumage; pale spot behind bill; pale blue upper wing coverts.

STATUS: Common migrant and breeder over all but the more arid areas of the region; rare in winter.

Long-distance migrants that winter as far away as Central America, Blue-winged Teal are one of the last ducks to arrive in spring and the first to head south in autumn. Upon arrival, they seek out small-shallow marshes, often surrounded by native prairie. There, they forage in the shallows on aquatic plants.

Pair-bonds are often formed during the spring migration and the pairs begin looking for a suitable small pond or flooded roadside ditch to establish their home range. The female chooses the nest site, typically on dry land near water. She lays eight to thirteen eggs, usually in May or June, in a grass-lined nest well hidden in foot-high vegetation.

Skilled fliers, groups of Blue-winged Teal in flight resemble squadrons of fighter planes on maneuvers in tight formation, gliding just above the marsh vegetation. The blue flash of their upper wing coverts narrows identification to either the Blue-winged Teal or its close relative, the Cinnamon Teal, which has a predominantly chestnut body color. The teal's fast flight and ability to change direction almost instantaneously provide a challenge to participants in the fall hunting season.

——SIMILAR SPECIES——

Green-winged Teal
Anas crecca

FIELD MARKS: 14 inches. *Male:* small; **chestnut head with a green patch from the eye to the nape; white vertical stripe up side of breast.** *Female:* brown plumage; white belly; green speculum.

STATUS: Summer resident in the Dakotas and the northern half of NE; rare winter resident.

The smallest of the North American dabbling ducks, Green-winged Teal prefer to winter in fresh water and so do not move all the way south to the waters of the Gulf Coast like the other teal. Highly social, Green-winged Teal often begin to display in late winter and continue until well into the spring. Like many of the other dabbling ducks, they have a wide variety of elaborate courtship displays that are very interesting to watch. Green-winged Teal nests are often located beneath low shrubs that provide overhead concealment. They show a stronger preference than other species for feeding on exposed mudflats.

Blue-winged Teal pair

Male Green-winged Teal

Cinnamon Teal   *Anas cyanoptera*

FIELD MARKS: 15 inches. *Male:* small; **cinnamon-colored plumage;** red eyes; **pale blue upper wing coverts.** *Female:* brown plumage; large, broad bill; no whitish spot behind bill like the female Blue-winged Teal.

STATUS: Rare resident and migrant in this region; more common further west.

While the dark cinnamon color of the male differs markedly from the blue head and brown body of the male Blue-winged Teal, Cinnamon Teal are remarkably similar to the Blue-winged Teal in many aspects of their appearance and behavior. The females of the two species are very difficult to distinguish from each other. Both species prefer small, shallow, grassy marshes, but Cinnamon Teal tend to choose drier or more alkaline areas. Cinnamon Teal also feed primarily on aquatic plants in shallow water, along the water's edge or on mudflats.

Male Cinnamon Teal

DIVING DUCKS

Redhead
Aythya americana

FIELD MARKS: 19 inches. *Male:* rusty red head; orange-yellow eyes; dish-faced profile; black breast and rump; gray back and sides. *Female:* brown plumage; round head; white belly.

STATUS: Fairly common migrant and breeder east of the BH and BLNP.

Like other diving ducks, Redheads prefer the open areas of fairly large bodies of water and feed by diving. Divers from this region winter in bays along the Gulf of Mexico, but move north to inland marshes in the Northern Great Plains region and further north in spring to nest. Most Redheads breed in the prairie potholes common in this region. The draining of these nesting ponds has permanently reduced the numbers of these and other pothole-nesting ducks.

Redhead females seem to prefer to build their nests in cattails or bulrushes from 20 to 40 inches high and in water about a foot deep. They lay from eight to fifteen eggs and incubate them on their own. Some females are rather careless with their eggs, laying them in the nests of other species, as well as constructing "dump" nests where several Redheads lay eggs but no one incubates them.

More vegetarian than other divers, Redheads frequent shallow lakes and marshes where they dive to depths of about 10 feet in pursuit of pondweed, their favorite food. In winter, Redheads keep company with other diving ducks, particularly scaup.

——SIMILAR SPECIES——

Canvasback
Aythya valisineria

FIELD MARKS: 20 inches. **Long, sloping forehead.** *Male:* chestnut red head; **red eye; white back and sides.** *Female:* brown plumage.

STATUS: More common in Canada; fairly common migrants throughout the Northern Great Plains and breeders in north-central NE, the eastern third of SD, and most of the eastern two-thirds of ND; less common in eastern MT and WY; does not breed in the BH or BLNP.

One of the largest of the diving ducks, "Cans"—as hunters affectionately call them—are also primarily vegetarian. Capable of diving to 30 feet, they most often feed on the tuberous roots of aquatic plants in 3 to 15 feet of water. Favored foods are wapatoo and pondweed. After breeding in the emergent vegetation surrounding small ponds and lakes, Canvasbacks congregate in great numbers on large lakes and reservoirs. Long, pointed wings carry these powerful fliers at speeds up to 60 miles per hour. As with many pothole-nesting ducks, population numbers suffer in drought years when their nesting ponds dry up.

Redhead pair

Male Canvasback

Female Canvasback

Lesser Scaup

Aythya affinis

FIELD MARKS: 12 inches. *Male:* pale blue bill with small, dark nail (projection) at tip; dark head, neck, and breast with a purple sheen; **peaked head profile;** barred gray back and sides; black rump. *Female:* brown plumage.

STATUS: Common to abundant migrant in the east; less common further west and in the BH.

Expert divers, Lesser Scaup prefer the less salty water of brackish bays and deep, freshwater reservoirs and lakes, where they feed almost exclusively on aquatic invertebrates. Pairs of these birds breed locally in this region mostly north and east of the Missouri River. There they seek out slightly brackish ponds with large numbers of invertebrates and aquatic insects. These ponds may be found in prairie marshes or in partially wooded parklands.

The pair-bond forms in winter and, as with most of the other divers, lasts until the eggs are laid, when the male abandons the incubating female. Nests are usually on dry land within 150 feet of water. Scaup nest relatively late, and the young may not hatch until July. In fall, the young and adults linger as far north as they can find open water. During mild winters, they may winter much further north than during normal winters.

----SIMILAR SPECIES----

Greater Scaup

Aythya marila

FIELD MARKS: 13 inches. *Male:* pale blue bill with dark tail; dark head, neck, and breast with a greenish sheen; **rounded head profile;** pale gray back and sides; black rump. *Female:* brown plumage.

STATUS: Rare to uncommon migrant, seen most often in the fall, in eastern NE and the Dakotas—particularly along the Missouri River.

In contrast to Lesser Scaup, which are often found on inland waters, Greater Scaup gather in flocks, often numbering in the thousands, on open bays or out on the open water where they dive for mollusks. They pass through this region in early April on their way to their nesting grounds across northern Canada.

Ring-necked Duck

Aythya collaris

FIELD MARKS: 12 inches. *Male:* **dark head, neck, and breast** with purple sheen; **white band on bill; black back;** gray sides. *Female:* gray brown plumage; gray bill with black tip and white ring; pale eye ring; steep forehead; peaked crown.

STATUS: Fairly common migrant through most of the region and resident breeder in suitable habitats in the northeastern parts of the Dakotas.

Woodland ponds ringed with stubbly growth are the preferred habitat of the Ring-necked Duck. Most Ring-necked Ducks only pass through this region on their way to the reedy borders of bogs and ponds in southern Canada, but some linger and nest here. Unlike many other divers, Ring-necked Ducks rarely use salt water and mingle less frequently with other species.

Male Lesser Scaup

Female Lesser Scaup

Male Greater Scaup

Ring-necked Duck
—Photo by Tom J. Ulrich

MERGANSERS

Common Merganser
Mergus merganser

FIELD MARKS: 24 inches. *Male:* long, low profile; black above; white below; **long, slender, hooked red bill; green head; red legs.** *Female:* dark chestnut head; gray plumage; **clear white throat.**

STATUS: Common migrant throughout the region; rare breeder along the Missouri River and in the BH; common in BLNP.

Common Mergansers prefer large, open streams and marshy bays. They search out nearby hollow trees or similarly well-protected cavities to protect their nests.

This adept swimmer feeds almost exclusively on small fish, locating them either by snorkeling (swimming with only the bill and eyes submerged) or by diving. Its slender, saw-toothed bill—the source of its nickname, Sawbill—is perfect for grasping slippery prey. When flushed, Common Mergansers must make a long, exhausting run across the surface of the water to gain enough speed to become airborne.

——SIMILAR SPECIES——

Northern Shoveler
Anas clypeata

FIELD MARKS: 19 inches. *Male:* large, dark, spatulate bill; green head; rusty sides; white chest; pale blue upper wing coverts. *Female:* large, spatulate bill; mottled brown coloration.

STATUS: Common summer resident throughout the region; less common in the west; migrant in the BH; uncommon in BLNP.

Although included here as a similar species because of its color pattern, the Northern Shoveler is actually much more similar to the teal in its habits than to the mergansers.

Northern Shovelers frequent shallow prairie marshes where they feed on tiny invertebrates in shallow water. Taking a bill full of bottom ooze, the "Spoonbill" swishes his bill from side to side, forcing water and liquid mud between the comb-like lamellae on the edges of the bill and leaving behind insect larvae, small crustaceans, seeds, and bits of plant material. Or, he may just swim slowly, with his neck extended, and use his bill to skim insects off the surface of the water. If suitable shallows are not available, Shovelers will also tip to feed like the other surface ducks.

Shovelers build their nests well away from the water, in grasses between one and two feet high. The female lays between eight and thirteen eggs in a shallow depression and incubates them on her own. The eggs hatch in about twenty-four days, and the young follow the mother to water almost immediately.

Male Common Merganser

Female Common Merganser

Male Northern Shoveler

STIFF-TAILED DUCKS

Ruddy Duck
Oxyura jamaicensis

FIELD MARKS: 15 inches. ***Male:*** deep rusty red body; **bright blue bill;** black cap; white cheeks; **long tail often carried pointing straight up.** ***Female:*** brownish color; whitish cheek patch; **long, often upturned tail.**

STATUS: Fairly common migrant and summer resident throughout the region, except in the area surrounding the BH, BLNP, and southeastern NE.

Members of this group of ducks are small, stubby, and have distinctively short necks. As the group name implies, the tail is often held up stiffly when swimming. They are expert divers, but can also submerge by sinking slowly into the water as some of the grebes commonly do.

Most common at lower elevations, Ruddy Ducks breed in ponds and lakes overgrown with vegetation. The preferred habitats seem to be permanent prairie marshes with relatively stable water levels and ringed with cattails or bulrushes. Open water must be near the emergent vegetation or at least be accessible through open channels of water.

After arriving in the spring, a male chooses a suitable area of the pond and begins to perform his unique "bubbling" courtship routine of beating his bill on his breast and producing a thumping-gurgling sound. The female selects a dense bulrush stand and begins construction of the nest by bending the bulrush stems over to form a platform or floating nest. Usually, the nest has a canopy over it and a ramp sloping down to the water for access.

The females lay unusually large eggs and commonly drop them in the nests of other ducks. A clutch may include from three to fifteen eggs, with the average being seven or eight. Although some males may hang around during the process, the female does the incubation. The precocial ducklings hatch in about twenty-three days. Highly independent, the young may scatter throughout the marsh before they are able to fly.

Like most other diving ducks, Ruddy Ducks winter along all our coastlines, although, unlike the scaup, they rarely winter in the Great Lakes. They are often in the company of other ducks and raft with a variety of other diving ducks.

Male Ruddy Duck

Female Ruddy Duck

Ruddy Duck displaying

PHEASANTS, GROUSE, TURKEYS, AND QUAIL
ORDER GALLIFORMES

Pheasants, Grouse, Turkeys, and Quail are heavy-bodied, chickenlike land birds. Their short, heavy bills have a decurved upper mandible, ideal for foraging on seeds and insects. They rely on their powerful legs to carry them out of danger as their short, rounded wings enable them to attain full flight speed with a couple wingbeats but do not allow sustained flight. The males are more colorful than the females and often engage in elaborate courtship displays. The courting male will strut; raise or spread specialized feathers on the head, neck, or tail; inflate air sacs in the neck; beat the air with his wings; or release air from specialized neck sacs to produce a variety of courtship sounds. Females nest on the ground and lay large clutches (ten to fourteen) of eggs, which they begin incubating after laying the last egg, so the eggs hatch together. The precocial young emerge covered with down and leave the nest almost immediately.

Pheasants and Partridge (Family Phasianidae), like the rest of the family, scratch the surface of the ground for seeds and insects. In contrast to the grouse, pheasants, quail, and partridge have nostrils and tarsi that are bare of feathers. In addition, these birds have bare patches of skin instead of inflatable air sacs for courtship displays. They use spurs on their lower legs for fighting.

Pheasants include the Ring-necked Pheasant, Chukar, and Gray Partridge. None of the birds in this group are native to the region or to North America, but were mainly introduced from the Far East.

Ring-necked Pheasant: rooster crowing

Grouse are medium-sized birds with moderate to long tails. Adapted to cold, snowy climates, grouse have feather-covered nostrils and feet. Lateral extensions of scales on their toes serve as "snowshoes" in winter. In early spring, the males attract females for breeding through elaborate courtship behaviors. The forest species usually display individually, while the open-country species gather on communal breeding grounds called leks.

Blue Grouse in Douglas-fir

*Wild Turkey
tom displaying*

Turkeys are large birds with naked heads, broad wings, long legs, and broad, fan-shaped tails. They feed on nuts and seeds.

Quail (Family Odontophoridae) are small, round-bodied birds with short tails and necks. Quail live in extended family groups, or coveys, of six to twenty birds most of the year, except during the nesting season.

Gray Partridge

PHEASANTS

Ring-necked Pheasant

Phasianus colchicus

FIELD MARKS: 33 inches. *Male:* large; **multicolored plumage;** white neck ring; long, tapered tail. *Female:* mottled brown plumage.

STATUS: Introduced from the Far East; resident in agricultural habitats throughout the region; not found in the coniferous habitats of the BH; rare in badlands of BLNP.

The success of the Ring-necked Pheasant is due in part to its widespread introduction. Ring-necked Pheasants were first introduced into this region near Sturgis, SD, in 1891 and then in Minnehaha County in 1899 and again in 1903. Since then, hunters have introduced this prized game bird to almost all suitable habitats.

Closely linked to agriculture, pheasants feed on weed seeds, insects, and waste grain. They nest in the weedy margins of agricultural cropland, as well as in grain and alfalfa fields. The male is polygamous and attracts hens in spring by beating his wings and crowing from a favored location within his home range. Each male may attract a harem of females who hang around until they have mated, when they leave to seek out a nest site.

Nests are located in thick vegetation still standing from the previous summer. Roadside ditches, fencerows, and similar patches of "waste" land are often used for nesting. Early-growing cropland, such as alfalfa fields, may also be used. Depending on the harvest schedule, hens nesting in these areas may be killed or, if they are fortunate, only have their nests destroyed by the mowing machines. If the female survives, she will often renest with better success.

Young have been reported as early as mid-May and as late as early September. Like other birds in this order, the young mature rapidly and can fly very short distances when only a week old. The young generally stay with the female for about six to eight weeks.

The young males begin to assume their adult plumage in early fall, just about in time for the fall hunting season (when only males are legal game). Although they spend summers alone or in small family groups, pheasants often form large flocks in late winter.

Pheasant hunting is a major industry in this region. In South Dakota alone, over 170,000 hunters took nearly 1.7 million Ring-necked Pheasants during the 2004 season. The 2004 preseason population in South Dakota was estimated at 8.1 million pheasants.

Male Ring-necked Pheasant

Ring-necked Pheasant crowing

Female Ring-necked Pheasant

GROUSE

Ruffed Grouse
Bonasa umbellus

FIELD MARKS: 17 inches. Brown and buff plumage; ragged "crest"; **breast and sides marked with dark V shapes;** fan-shaped, barred tail with dark subterminal band, tarsi feathered to the feet.

STATUS: Uncommon permanent resident in extreme southeastern ND and in the BH; not found in BLNP.

HOT SPOTS: Strawberry Lake, Bottineau, ND; Black Hills, SD.

The most widely distributed grouse in the United States, the Ruffed Grouse inhabits deciduous woodlands and also mixed coniferous forests that include a mixture of aspen, poplars, and birches. This species prefers brushy habitats adjacent to open farmlands or with numerous small openings. There, it feeds on berries, buds, leaves, and needles. In summer it supplements its diet with insects, which it picks from the surface of the ground.

As the snow disappears in spring, males seek out a large fallen log that will become the platform for their courtship displays. The prominent log is usually located beneath the canopy of a mixed stand of large trees. The male grips a favored spot on the log with his claws and beats his wings rapidly, producing a muffled thumping sound not unlike that of a distant drum. This "drumming" sound is produced by changes in air pressure generated by the beating wings rather than by the wings striking the breast or each other. Other Ruffed Grouse, hearing the sound, approach the log. The resident bird then begins an elaborate ritualized strutting display, raising the ruffs on its neck that give it its name. If the bird is another male, a fight may ensue. If the approaching bird is a female, copulation may result. After mating, the female builds a nest, often at the base of a large hardwood tree, where she deposits her clutch of eleven or twelve eggs.

——SIMILAR SPECIES——

Blue Grouse
Dendragapus obscurus

FIELD MARKS: 18 inches. *Male:* uniform gray plumage; square, **black, fan-shaped tail with gray terminal band.** *Female:* brownish plumage.

STATUS: Extirpated over most of this region, the eastern edge of current range in MT and WY extends almost to the BH; not found in BLNP.

The typical grouse of coniferous forests, the Blue Grouse, or "Fool Hen," is extremely tolerant of human disturbance. Early settlers are said to have killed these birds for food using only sticks and stones. In spring, males attract the females by "hooting." The polygamous males expose a reddish patch of neck skin surrounded by a ring of white feathers. Their eye combs act as barometers of their psychological state—yellow when calm, red when excited or disturbed. Blue Grouse nest in open foothills and the broods follow ripening berry patches up the mountainside. They move upslope in winter to Douglas-fir thickets just below the timberline, where they are sustained by the plentiful supply of needles.

Ruffed Grouse —Photo by Tom J. Ulrich
Inset: *Ruffed Grouse chick*

Blue Grouse

Greater Prairie-Chicken   *Tympanuchus cupido*

FIELD MARKS: 14 inches. Barred brown above; short, rounded, blackish tail. ***Displaying males:* orange air sacs.**

STATUS: Once found throughout the region; now local in areas of virgin prairie; not found in the BH or BLNP.

HOT SPOTS: Fort Niobrara and Valentine NWRs, NE; Fort Pierre NG, SD; Sheyenne NG, ND; Tamarack Ranch SWA, CO.

Prairie-chickens are found in native grasslands or in mixed habitats of grassland and cropland in which the grasslands are the dominant habitat type.

Greater Prairie-Chickens are most easily seen in spring when the males gather on communal leks or booming grounds to perform their territorial and courtship displays. Each morning, often from March through May, the males make their way in the predawn darkness to their small territory in the lek to display. As the day dawns, the males strut about their territory, puffing out their bright orange neck sacs and producing a "booming" sound. The "master cocks," the dominant males near the center of the lek, are the ones found most attractive by the hens; consequently those males do most of the breeding.

The female then departs and lays her daily egg in the nesting site of her choice. She returns again and again until the entire clutch is laid and she begins incubation. As with other gallinaceous birds, the precocial chicks hatch together and are brooded by the female for a few days. They can fly short distances in less than two weeks.

Loss of their native habitat is the main problem facing Greater Prairie-Chickens. Several national wildlife refuges and national grasslands are preserving islands of the necessary grasslands and are the best places to observe these very interesting birds.

------SIMILAR SPECIES------
Sharp-tailed Grouse   *Tympanuchus phasianellus*

FIELD MARKS: 18 inches. Brown and buff plumage; **breast and sides marked with dark Vs; pointed tail. *Displaying males:* purple air sacs.**

STATUS: Resident breeder throughout most of the region except southern and southeastern NE and the forested areas of the BH.

HOT SPOTS: Arrowwood, Lostwood, and Long Lake NWRs, ND; Crescent Lake and Fort Niobrara NWRs, NE; Medicine Lake NWR, MT.

Mainly a prairie grouse, the Sharp-tailed Grouse inhabits grasslands interspersed with limited brushy cover. Before dawn on April mornings, the males gather to "dance" on traditional courting grounds, or leks, where they wheel around like wind-up toys. The dancing establishes a hierarchy among the males. The oldest and largest males occupy the territories in the center and do the majority of the breeding. Sharp-tails require native grasslands, so as grasslands disappear, so will the Sharp-tails.

Male Greater Prairie-Chicken displaying —Photo by Tom J. Ulrich

Sharp-tailed Grouse dancing

Greater Sage-Grouse   *Centrocercus urophasianus*

FIELD MARKS: *Male:* 32 inches; *Female:* 21 inches. Grayish brown above; blackish below; long pointed tail. ***Displaying males:* white neck and chest with yellow air sacs, spiky fanned tail.**

STATUS: Limited to the sagebrush habitats of eastern MT, WY, and extreme western ND and SD.

HOT SPOTS: Charles M. Russell NWR, MT; Big Gumbo and Limber Pines, Marmarth, ND.

As its name implies, this grouse only lives in sagebrush country. Unlike the other members of the order that have tough, muscular gizzards to aid in digesting hard seeds and grain, sage-grouse have soft, membranous gizzards—indicative of their softer diet of the buds and leaves of sagebrush, supplemented with insects during the summer brood-rearing period. In spring, sixty or more males may gather on a single lek to boom and display. Destruction of sagebrush habitat and booming grounds are the main factors causing the slow but steady decline of this species.

Male Greater Sage-Grouse displaying

TURKEYS

Wild Turkey *Meleagris gallopavo*

FIELD MARKS: *Male:* 48 inches; *Female:* 36 inches. **Large size;** dark, iridescent plumage; large fan-shaped tail tipped with buff; **naked head.**

STATUS: Common in the BH, uncommon in BLNP; local elsewhere as a result of introductions.

HOT SPOTS: Fort Niobrara NWR, Valentine, NE (viewing blind).

Lewis and Clark, in their journals, wrote about seeing turkeys along the main channel and tributaries of the Missouri River. However, shortly after that, early settlers extirpated these birds from the region. In 1948 reintroduction of Wild Turkeys began in the Black Hills. The birds found the ponderosa pine forests and mixed woods along streams and rivers to their liking and began to multiply and disperse. Since then, three subspecies of Wild Turkeys (Merriam's in the Black Hills, and Eastern and Rio Grande in the east) have been reintroduced into almost every suitable habitat throughout the region, primarily bottomlands along the rivers and streams of the region, and are now one of the main game birds in the region.

When encountering danger, turkeys prefer to rely on their powerful legs to carry them out of danger. However, when startled, a few strokes of their short rounded wings enable them to attain full flight speed and carry them quickly out of danger. However, while powerful, their wings do not allow sustained flight. Consequently, turkeys do not migrate.

Highly gregarious, Wild Turkeys move about in flocks except when the hens scatter to nest in the spring. Courtship is both interesting and obvious. The colorful toms follow the groups of hens, strutting, and raising and spreading their specialized tail feathers. The "gobblers" also force blood into their naked wattles, changing them from gray-blue to a bloodred color. The toms then stretch out their necks and "gobble." Before the first gobble has subsided, virtually every other gobbler within hearing distance also sounds off. During the spring season, toms will gobble in response to virtually any loud sound—a characteristic routinely used by hunters to locate these birds.

After the courtship, the hen builds a nest on the ground, well hidden in overhanging vegetation, and lays a large clutch of ten to fourteen eggs. The male plays no role in nest building, incubation, or raising the young. The precocial young hatch covered with down and leave the nest almost immediately.

Male Wild Turkey

Female Wild Turkey

Male Wild Turkey displaying

QUAIL

Northern Bobwhite
Colinus virginianus

FIELD MARKS: 9 inches. Small, stocky; brownish above; streaked sides; grayish and scaled below. *Male:* **black cap and eye line; white throat and over-eye line.** *Female:* brown cap and eye line; buffy throat and over-eye line.

STATUS: Resident breeder in southeastern NE, and extending up the river systems into southeastern SD and eastern CO and WY; not found in the BH or BLNP.

This region is the extreme northwestern extent of the Northern Bobwhite's range. More at home in the habitats of the southeastern United States, the Bobwhite is the only quail native to this region.

Inhabitants of "edge" habitats, Northern Bobwhites require a number of elements to survive: they need cultivated crops for a reliable food source, brushy undergrowth for escape cover, grassy fields for nesting, a water source, and dry areas for dusting. In this region habitats lining the waterways are basically the only habitats that provide all these elements.

As winter fades, males choose a singing post from which they declare their sexual availability by uttering their familiar *"bob-bob-white"* call. Unlike some of the other gallinaceous birds, bobwhites usually form monogamous pairs and both sexes seek out a nest site and build the nest. One egg is laid each day until the clutch of up to twenty eggs is laid. The male does not help with incubation unless the female is killed. The young grow rapidly and can fly short distances within two weeks.

Family bonds remain intact through the fall, with members forming coveys of six or more birds. Individual birds or unsuccessful nesting pairs join other groups. Coveys settle into a circular roosting formation to conserve heat on cold winter nights. When disturbed, the entire covey usually bursts into flight at the same time.

———SIMILAR SPECIES———

Gray Partridge
Perdix perdix

FIELD MARKS: 12 inches. **Orange brown face;** gray back and breast; brown belly. *In flight:* **rusty tail.**

STATUS: Introduced; locally abundant in irrigated farmlands, primarily in ND, the northern half of SD, and eastern MT and WY; not found in the BH; rare in BLNP.

Although it resembles a quail, the Gray Partridge is more closely related to the pheasants than to the quail. Gray Partridge show a stronger preference for agricultural fields than do Northern Bobwhite, and, like the bobwhite, are found in coveys all year except during the nesting season. Because they prefer dense cover, Gray Partridge are seldom seen except during the fall and winter when snow covers their hiding places, forcing them to congregate along roads and in open fields. When disturbed, the entire covey flushes at once in a noisy explosion of beating wings and hoarse calls. The covey stays together in flight until it drops out of sight on a nearby knoll or ridge. Gray Partridge often roost in a circle on the ground, like bobwhites, or plunge into a soft snowdrift to spend cold winter nights.

Northern Bobwhite —Photo by Tom J. Ulrich

Gray Partridge —Photo by Alan G. Nelson

LOONS
ORDER GAVIIFORMES

Loons (Family Gaviidae) are large, heavy diving birds. Webbed feet and legs located well back on their bodies make them strong swimmers but render them almost helpless on land. They submerge either by diving forward or by sinking out of sight, and may swim 50 to 100 yards underwater before resurfacing. They rarely come ashore except during nesting season.

Common Loon —Photo by Tom J. Ulrich

GREBES
ORDER PODICIPEDIFORMES

Grebes (Family Podicipedidae) are swimming and diving birds with long necks and inconspicuous tails. Legs set well back on their bodies and lobed toes make them excellent swimmers but clumsy walkers. Grebes feed primarily on fish and small aquatic animals. They engage in elaborate courtship displays accompanied by a variety of wails and whistles before building their floating nests of emergent plants in shallow water near shore. Slight differences in bill size distinguish the sexes. Young grebes often ride on their parents' backs, tucked safely under the wing coverts. Sometimes the young remain there even while the adult dives; other times, they pop up like corks soon after the adult submerges.

Horned Grebe

Pied-billed Grebe

Eared Grebe

Red-necked Grebe and chick

LOONS

Common Loon *Gavia immer*

FIELD MARKS: 32 inches. Long, flat profile; **black head;** heavy, daggerlike black bill; red eyes; white necklace; **black back densely checkered with small white spots;** yodeling call.

STATUS: Uncommon migrant in the eastern part of the region; most often seen in the northeast and along the Missouri River.

HOT SPOTS: Bowdoin and Charles M. Russell NWRs, MT; Bonny Reservoir, CO.

Nothing embodies the spirit of the wilderness quite as well as the haunting predawn cry of a Common Loon echoing across the mist-shrouded waters of a dead-calm lake. In fact, it is their distinctive, yodel-like, wailing laugh that often provides the first clue to their presence. While the call is given most frequently during the breeding season as a territorial announcement, the plaintive cry can be heard occasionally during other seasons on those mysterious, calm, foggy days.

Common Loons pause to rest and feed on the larger lakes of this region on their way to and from their wintering areas along the Gulf Coast and their breeding grounds, which stretch from Minnesota north to the Arctic. Although they are relatively strong fliers, they require a long run on open water to become airborne. Upon their arrival in the north, loons seek out suitable nest sites on the shores of lakes with abundant small fish and crustaceans.

Because loons hunt primarily by sight, they are most often found on clear water lakes. Loons often hunt by swimming slowly along the surface with their bill and eyes submerged. If prey is spotted, they dive—often catching the prey relatively close to the surface. However, when necessary, loons can dive to depths of 200 feet or more. The daggerlike bill, in spite of its appearance, is used to grasp their prey, not to spear it.

Courtship involves synchronous displays between the male and female and involves swimming, diving, and chasing. The mounded nest is built on land but within a couple feet of the water so the adult can slip off into the water in response to any disturbance. Two eggs are laid and the young take to the water soon after hatching. Both adults participate in feeding the young and the young often ride on the backs of the adults.

Solitude is crucial to the breeding success of loons, and, at present, their numbers appear to be declining primarily because of disturbance of their nesting areas by humans.

Common Loon —Photo by Tom J. Ulrich

Common Loon with chicks —Photo by Tom J. Ulrich

GREBES

Western Grebe   *Aechmophorus occidentalis*

FIELD MARKS: 25 inches. **Long, slim, black-and-white neck;** long, sharp, green-yellow bill; **black cap extends below the eye;** black on back of neck is wider than the stripe on the Clark's Grebe.

STATUS: Summer resident throughout the northern and western part of the region; rare in eastern NE.

Western Grebes dive from the surface of the water and may remain under-water from ten to forty seconds while pursuing fish and small aquatic animals. Western Grebes swallow a large number of their own feathers, which they pick from their bellies and flanks. Scientists believe the feathers may protect the grebe's stomach lining from indigestible parts of the fish they eat. The feathers also provide additional bulk that allows the grebes to regurgitate pellets made up of the indigestible parts of their prey. This regurgitation process may also aid in removing parasites from their digestive tracts.

Western Grebes engage in elaborate courtship displays, which are accompanied by a variety of wails and whistles. With heads low and crests erect, the male and female swim toward each other. They dip their beaks into the water and shake their heads vigorously from side to side. Then they turn sideways, raise upright, arch their wings and necks back in a graceful curve, and simultaneously rush over the surface of the water. Suddenly they dive, only to reappear seconds later to swim calmly side by side.

The floating nests are often built in loose colonies, constructed of a mass of vegetation and anchored in shallow water near shore. The chicks are able to swim and dive as soon as they hatch. They are fed small fish and invertebrates by the adults. The young grebes often ride on their parents' backs, tucked safely under the wing coverts. They may remain there even while the adult dives.

Most Western Grebes move to the coasts for the winter, often feeding far out in open water. With the coming of spring, they move inland again in search of the larger freshwater marshes they use for breeding.

——SIMILAR SPECIES——

Clark's Grebe   *Aechmophorus clarkii*

FIELD MARKS: 22 inches. **Long, slim, black-and-white neck;** long, sharp, orange-yellow bill; **white cheek extends above the eye.** More white on sides just above the waterline than the Western Grebe.

STATUS: Summer resident in eastern WY; rare further east.

HOT SPOTS: Sand Lake NWR, SD.

Clark's Grebes inhabit the same sloughs and shallow marshes preferred by Western Grebes, although the Clark's Grebes tend to forage further from shore and in deeper water than Western Grebes. Once considered by ornithologists to be a separate species, then a color morph of the Western Grebe, Clark's Grebe is once again considered a separate species.

Western Grebe

PELICANS AND CORMORANTS
ORDER PELECANIFORMES

Pelicans (Family Pelecanidae) are large, aquatic, fish-eating birds with over-sized bills and large gular (throat) pouches that they use to catch and carry fish. Large feet with webs between all four toes help propel them through the water. Pelicans are monogamous, but the pair-bond only lasts for a single breeding season. White pelicans nest on the ground but may construct a size-able mound of vegetation and debris. Two or three eggs make up the normal clutch and both adults participate in the incubation. Pelicans do not have a brood patch, so the eggs are incubated on the feet. The eggs hatch one per day, in the order in which they were laid. The newly hatched young are fed a regurgitated "soup" by both parents. As they get older, the youngsters begin to reach into the adults' gullets for partially digested fish. After about thirty days, the young band together and form huge "crèches," a behavior that is believed to help with temperature regulation and protection against predators.

White Pelican

Cormorants (Family Phalacrocoracidae) are heavy bodied, primarily black birds that swim low in the water with their bill tilted upward. They dive from the surface, sometimes to depths of several hundred feet, and swim underwater in pursuit of fish. They have gular pouches similar to, but much smaller than, those of the pelicans. Their sharply hooked bill enables them to grasp and hold their slippery prey.

Double-crested Cormorant

Double-crested Cormorant

PELICANS

American White Pelican *Pelecanus erythrorhynchos*

FIELD MARKS: 60 inches. **Large, flat, orange bill;** large throat patch; white plumage with black wing tips.

STATUS: Locally common breeder and fairly common migrant throughout the region; not found in the BH; occasional in BLNP.

HOT SPOTS: Bowdoin and Medicine Lake NWRs, MT; Riverside Reservoir, CO; J. Clark Salyer and Chase Lake NWRs, ND; Lacreek and Waubay NWRs, SD; Valentine NWR, NE.

With wings spanning 9 feet, American White Pelicans are the largest birds in the region. Primarily fish eaters, White Pelicans feed by swimming on the surface of the water and submerging their heads to scoop up fish in their large bills. In addition to the fish, the large gular pouch may "capture" up to 3 gallons of water. They press the pouch against their throat to expel the water before swallowing the fish.

Groups of White Pelicans may fish cooperatively by forming a line and moving slowly through the water, extending their bills beneath the water and capturing fish as they go. Often, they paddle and extend their heads and bills in unison to capture the fish they disturb. Groups of pelicans may also form a line and "herd" fish into shallow water where they are more easily captured. Other times, two groups of pelicans may move toward each other, forcing the fish into the narrowing space between the two lines.

Although the pouch is mainly a fish-catching device, it contains a rich supply of blood vessels and is used in warm weather to dissipate body heat. To accomplish this, the pelicans "flutter" the pouch to create air movement and speed the transmission of heat. Observers near breeding colonies on hot days will see almost the entire colony of birds performing this gular flutter to stay cool.

During the breeding season, a horny growth forms on the top of the bill of both sexes and the colors of the pouch intensify, factors that are believed to have a function during courtship. After bonding, the pairs gather on isolated islands in large lakes, where they nest in colonies. The largest breeding colony in the region is at Chase Lake National Wildlife Refuge in North Dakota.

Adults may leave the nesting colony in orderly lines, flying low over the water, and go 100 miles or more to reach feeding waters with enough fish to meet the needs of the youngsters. In years of inadequate food, the youngest, weakest chicks may be pushed aside by the older, stronger siblings at feeding time, providing a mechanism for the survival of at least some of the youngsters.

American White Pelican populations now appear to be stable after recovering from the effects of DDT and other chemical contamination of their food supply. However, year-to-year fluctuations still occur and protection of their food supply and nesting islands will continue to be necessary.

American White Pelican

American White Pelican

American White Pelicans

EGRETS, HERONS, BITTERNS, AND VULTURES
ORDER CICONIIFORMES

Egrets, Herons, and Bitterns (Family Ardeidae) are long-legged wading birds with long necks and long, straight, daggerlike bills. Most nest in colonies and develop long plumes, or aigrettes, during the breeding season. The pairs use a number of highly ritualized displays to cement the pair-bond, including *twig-passing, bill-stroking* and *feather-nibbling.* The male brings the materials for building the nest and the female does the actual construction. Both sexes share incubation and the feeding of the young. Herons are easily recognized in flight as they fly with deliberate wing beats, heads drawn back and legs extended.

Great Blue Heron with gar

Snowy Egret

American Bittern

White-faced Ibis   *Turkey Vulture*

Ibises (Family Threskiornithidae) are separated from the herons and egrets by their thin, decurved or flat, spoon-shaped bills. In addition, their wing beats are rapid, and they fly with their necks extended. Ibises move about actively in pursuit of food and often nest in mixed colonies with herons and egrets.

New World Vultures (Family Cathartidae) use their broad wings to soar effortlessly for hours on rising thermals, searching the landscape for carrion. Resembling hawks and eagles in many ways, they have naked heads, which are believed to be easier to keep clean when feeding on carcasses than a feathered head would be. The AOU has recently moved the New World vultures from the Order Falconiformes (hawks, eagles, and falcons) to the Order Ciconiiformes, which includes storks. While the reclassification is not universally accepted, most ornithologists believe it to be accurate based on morphological, behavioral, and DNA evidence.

Egrets, Herons, and Bitterns

Great Blue Heron
Ardea herodias

FIELD MARKS: 52 inches. **Large;** long yellow bill; **bluish gray color;** black crown stripe and crest.

STATUS: Common resident throughout the region along lakes, rivers, and reservoirs.

The largest, most common, and most visible heron in the region, Great Blue Herons frequent the shores and shallows of fresh water and, occasionally, upland meadows. As you might have guessed since they have the longest legs of the herons, they venture into the deepest water, often wading chest deep in search of prey. There, they often stand motionless until an unsuspecting fish, frog, or snake ventures by. When prey is spotted, the bird leans forward, inching closer and closer until the "coiled" neck strikes out and the knifelike bill skewers or catches the prey. They hunt small rodents in a similar way.

Great Blue Herons usually nest in colonies where suitable large trees are available. The nests are often placed in close proximity to each other, although out of range of the bills of the closest pair. The nests may be placed up to 100 feet above the ground, and the colonies often return to the same rookery and reuse the old nests year after year. They add new nesting material to the old nest each year, often resulting in massive nests. These colonies are often found in close association with cormorants, especially where the rising waters of impoundments have flooded and killed large trees suitable for nesting. Occasionally, Great Blues may nest on the ground on isolated islands.

——SIMILAR SPECIES——

Snowy Egret
Egretta thula

FIELD MARKS: 24 inches. Small size; all-white plumage; **black bill; black legs; yellow feet;** plumed head during the breeding season.

STATUS: Local breeders in the region; not found in the BH; rare in BLNP.

HOT SPOTS: Sand Lake NWR, SD.

These small, agile egrets prefer shallow marshes where they stir the bottom muck with one golden foot and then use their sharp bill to nab the small fish and crustaceans they disturb. They may also wait in ambush, stalk slowly through the shallows, or venture to the uplands in pursuit of grasshoppers and other insects.

Cattle Egret
Bubulcus ibis

FIELD MARKS: 20 inches. Small size; white plumage; **yellow bill; yellow-pink legs and feet;** buff orange crest, breast, and back during breeding season.

STATUS: Local breeders in the region; not found in the BH.

HOT SPOTS: Sand Lake NWR, SD.

An Old World bird, Cattle Egrets first appeared in the southeastern United States in 1952. They rapidly worked their way north and west and reached this region in the 1970s. Not bound to wetlands like other herons and egrets, the Cattle Egret more frequently accompanies livestock in dry pastures, where it feeds on grasshoppers and other insects disturbed by the grazing animals.

Great Blue Heron

Snowy Egret
Inset: *Cattle Egret*

Black-crowned Night-Heron *Nycticorax nycticorax*

FIELD MARKS: 25 inches. Small, stocky shape; black crown and back; red eyes; **black back;** grayish sides and breast; short legs; immature birds are heavily streaked, brownish gray.

STATUS: Fairly common local breeder throughout the region except in drier habitats.

True to their name, night-herons work the night shift, taking over the prime feeding areas at dusk when the other herons are returning to their night roosts. Large eyes enable them to see in the dim light as they stalk slowly through the shallows in pursuit of frogs, fish, and small crustaceans, which they dispatch with a lightning-quick strike. When foraging, Black-crowned Night Herons tend to crouch and almost appear to lack a neck. They may also hunt from ambush, standing motionless until an unsuspecting creature ventures within reach. Black-crowned Night Herons are well known for taking the chicks and eggs of other waterbirds—terns, ibises, and other herons.

After arriving in the region about mid-April, the males begin to establish territories. Usually found near other herons, the colonies of night-herons may be located on dry ground, in bulrush or cattail marshes, or in trees over 100 feet high. The males defend the territories with a variety of displays, eventually allowing a female to enter the territory. Mutual displays such as nibbling and billing help form the pair-bond, and the female then begins to complete the nest started by the male.

Fall migration peaks about mid-October, with the heavily streaked juveniles joining the adults as they move south and east to spend the winter. Totally at home in fresh, brackish, and salt water, night-herons spend their winters along southern rivers and the Atlantic and Gulf Coasts.

——SIMILAR SPECIES——

American Bittern *Botaurus lentiginosus*

FIELD MARKS: 28 inches. Moderate size; stocky shape; long, yellow bill; long neck with bold black stripe; brown streaked plumage.

STATUS: Fairly common summer resident throughout the region; rare in the BH and in BLNP.

This secretive marsh and bog dweller frequents the heavy vegetation bordering beaver ponds and marshes. Unlike the other herons, which feed mostly in open water, the solitary bittern prefers to feed among rushes. When startled, it freezes—neck and beak extended skyward, streaked breast blending beautifully with the surrounding rushes—and seems to disappear before your eyes. Although difficult to see, it is easy to hear. Its unmistakable call, a loud, low, pumping noise, seems to reverberate through the marsh.

Black-crowned Night-Heron

American Bittern

NEW WORLD VULTURES

Turkey Vulture
Cathartes aura

FIELD MARKS: 29 inches. Black body; small, naked, reddish head. ***In flight:*** **uptilted wings;** wings black in front, gray behind.

STATUS: Fairly common summer resident primarily west of the Missouri River, including the BH.

HOT SPOTS: Pine Ridge area of NE; Black Hills, SD; Teddy Roosevelt NP, ND.

These large, black birds winter across the southern United States and Mexico. In spring they begin their northward migration and arrive in this region in late March and April.

Usually seen high overhead, circling effortlessly on uptilted wings as they ride the rising masses of warm air called thermals. Because thermals are largely associated with fairly steep changes in topography, these birds can usually be found foraging around mountains and steep, deep waterways.

Because Turkey Vultures have a well-developed sense of smell, the thermals may help them locate their next meal by carrying the scent of carrion. Turkey Vultures also have very keen eyes and are believed to be able to distinguish a carcass from over two miles in the air. No sooner has the first vulture dropped from the sky than more appear, seemingly out of nowhere, to join in the meal. Their heavy bills allow them to tear off bite-sized pieces of the carcass to swallow.

To become airborne, Turkey Vultures must make a short run on the ground to generate some speed. This problem becomes even more acute when weighed down by a full belly.

Not a lot is known about their courtship or breeding behavior. Nests are usually located in a crevice or under an overhanging cliff. The two eggs are laid directly on the ground or in a small depression. Both sexes incubate and the young hatch after about forty days. Adults feed the young by regurgitating their last meal. The young develop slowly and fledge in about ten weeks.

Turkey Vulture

Young Turkey Vultures in nest cave

OSPREYS, HAWKS, EAGLES, AND FALCONS
ORDER FALCONIFORMES

Ospreys, Hawks, Eagles, and Falcons are the diurnal raptors, birds of prey that hunt by day and feed on flesh. Most of these birds have strong legs and feet, long, curved talons for grasping and killing live prey, and strong, heavy, hooked beaks for tearing the prey into bite-sized pieces. A few members of this family are scavengers. In most species, the females are generally larger than, but otherwise similar to, the males.

Hawks and Eagles (Family Accipitridae) are all excellent fliers with strong legs and powerful talons. They lack the characteristic notch in the beak common to the falcons.

Ospreys (Family Pandionidae) are fish eaters and consequently are invariably found near water. They were formerly classified in their own family based on some unique characteristics, including a reversible toe that allows them to grasp their slippery prey with two toes on each side of the fish.

Osprey

Accipiters (subfamily Accipitrinae) are small to medium-sized hawks that hunt in heavy woodlands and feed mainly on birds. Their short, rounded wings and long tails give them the speed and maneuverability they need when pursuing small birds through dense woods. In open flight, they alternate flapping and gliding. Females are generally larger than males.

Accipiter: Sharp-shinned Hawk

Buteo:
Rough-legged Hawk

Buteos (subfamily Accipitrinae) are medium to large soaring hawks that frequent open country. Broad, rounded wings and wide, fan-shaped tails allow them to soar almost motionless on thermals and expend very little energy while searching for prey. Buteos spot their prey from high overhead and then pursue it from a steep dive. Several of these species have two color morphs, one dark and one light, which complicates identification.

Eagles are similar to, but much larger than, buteos. Like the soaring hawks, they have broad wings and tails. Our two eagle species, although not closely related to each other, both feed on a wide variety of prey as well as carrion. Eagles pair for life and return to the same territory year after year. Pair-bonds are renewed each year with spectacular courtship displays, including locked-talon cartwheels that begin high in the air and spin toward the earth with breathtaking speed. A nesting pair of eagles usually raises one to three young each year if the food supply is sufficient.

Falcons (Family Falconidae), with their notched beaks, long, pointed wings, and long, slender tails, are strong, fast fliers. These streamlined birds inhabit open country and locate their prey from a vantage point high in the air and overtake it by means of a long, steep dive.

Prairie Falcon

EAGLES

Bald Eagle
Haliaeetus leucocephalus

FIELD MARKS: 31 inches. ***Adults:*** dark plumage; white head and tail; heavy yellow bill. ***Immature:*** dark plumage with white "armpits." ***In flight:*** underwing coverts lighter than flight feathers; tarsi not feathered to the toes.

STATUS: Endangered species. Uncommon migrant throughout the region; local common winter resident along the Missouri River below the reservoirs and in the BH; local breeder, particularly along the major rivers in eastern MT; uncommon in BLNP.

HOT SPOTS: Garrison Dam, Riverdale, ND; Devils Lake, ND; Karl Mundt and Sand Lake NWRs, SD; Lake Ogallala, NE; Johnson No. 2 Hydro Plant, Lexington, NE; Jackson Lake SP, CO.

Chosen in 1789 as our national symbol, this striking bird did not receive legal protection for another 150 years, when the National Emblem Act of 1940, also known as the Bald Eagle Protection Act, was passed. The white head and tail, the most easily recognizable characteristics of adult Bald Eagles, do not appear until the bird reaches four years of age. Bald Eagles feed mostly on fish, waterfowl, and carrion. They are usually found near fertile lakes and rivers that support an abundance of nongame fish such as suckers and squawfish, which the eagles snatch from shallow water with their sharp talons. Not above piracy, Bald Eagles will harry a fish-laden Osprey into dropping its booty, which the eagle then snags out of midair and carries to a perch to eat.

Their position at the top of the food chain makes Bald Eagles susceptible to contaminants that build up in their prey. Once critically threatened by DDT, Bald Eagle populations are recovering across the country. This recovery can be seen in this region primarily in winter when large numbers of these birds congregate below the dams and along the free-flowing sections of the Missouri River. There they feed on fish and sick or injured waterfowl. Carrion often takes the form of animals killed by collisions with cars; the slow-rising eagles are themselves susceptible to collisions with fast-moving vehicles.

Some Bald Eagles may nest in the extreme northeastern part of the region, where they choose tall trees near water.

——SIMILAR SPECIES——

Golden Eagle
Aquila chrysaetos

FIELD MARKS: 30 inches. ***Adults:*** large size; dark plumage; **golden cast to hind neck (at all ages);** fully feathered tarsi; ***in flight:*** large size; dark plumage; large, broad wings. ***Immature:*** dark plumage with some white spots; ***immature in flight:*** dark plumage; **white "wrist" spots; broad white tail band** with black tip.

STATUS: Fairly common resident in the western part of the region and in the BH and BLNP.

HOT SPOTS: Teddy Roosevelt NP, ND; Pawnee Buttes, CO.

Golden Eagles inhabit arid, open country broken by mountain ridges, grassland buttes, or semidesert canyons, where they place their large nests in trees or on cliffs. They feed mostly on mammals—ground squirrels, rabbits, and marmots. They will also take birds, and in winter often feed on carrion. As with other raptors, persecution by humans, pesticide contamination, and elimination of prey by habitat alteration are the main factors limiting its numbers.

Bald Eagle with carrion

Bald Eagle

Golden Eagle

HAWKS

Northern Harrier

Circus cyaneus

FIELD MARKS: *Male:* 18 inches; slim shape; **silvery gray;** *Female:* 22 inches; slim; **dark brown.** *In flight:* long, narrow, uplifted wings; white rump; flies low over the ground; sometimes hovers.

STATUS: Fairly common migrant and summer resident throughout the region and in BLNP; rare or absent in the BH.

As their former common name, "Marsh Hawk," implied, these birds are often associated with wet habitats. However, they are not limited to prairie marshes, as they also hunt and nest in many open habitats, including native grasslands, wet meadows, and some croplands in the vicinity of grasslands. They can often be seen flying buoyantly, usually quartering low over marshy habitat in search of mice, voles, frogs, or snakes. In areas with sparse vegetation, they hunt by sight. In taller, denser habitats, they can also hunt by sound, using their facial discs, similar to those of owls, to focus sound and pinpoint the location of prey.

The male arrives in the region before the female, usually in the last couple weeks of March. Courtship displays involve a variety of spectacular dives and swoops. During courtship, the pair may perform these maneuvers together, as well as lock talons in the air. Northern Harriers may nest in marshes, locating their nests over the water, in emergent vegetation along the shore, or in the uplands, where they utilize clumps of shrubs to conceal their activities. The nest is constructed of a variety of sticks, twigs, and grasses, and consists of little more than a small platform in which to lay the four to six eggs.

Incubation may begin at any time during the egg laying, resulting in chicks of different ages. The male brings food to the female during incubation and the early stages of brooding. The female, always alert, sees him coming and leaves the nest to meet him. He drops the food item, which she often catches in midair, and she immediately returns to the nest. As they grow and mature, the young begin to scatter into the surrounding vegetation, returning to the nest platform only when the female returns with food.

In mid-September, Northern Harriers move south, spending the cold winter months from the southern part of this region down to South America.

——SIMILAR SPECIES——

Osprey

Pandion haliaetus

FIELD MARKS: 24 inches. Predominantly white; broad black cheek line; black back. *In flight:* long, white wings bent at the wrist; **black wrist markings.**

STATUS: Uncommon migrant in the region; breeds just east of the region in Minnesota and just west of the region in MT and WY.

HOT SPOTS: Grove Lake WMA, Royal, NE; Lake Metigoshe SP, Bottineau, ND.

Superficially resembling the male Northern Harrier, Ospreys frequent clear lakes and streams where fish are plentiful. The bird spots a fish from the air, then dives feetfirst into the water to nab its catch. The Osprey carries the fish, with the head turned forward, to a perch to eat.

Male Northern Harrier —Photo by Tom J. Ulrich
Inset: *Female Northern Harrier* —Photo by Tom J. Ulrich

Osprey in flight
Inset: *Osprey*

Red-tailed Hawk
Buteo jamaicensis

FIELD MARKS: 21 inches. *In flight:* **rusty tail**; long, broad wings; wings whitish except for dark leading edge from body to a dark crescent at the wrist; fan-shaped tail. *Perched:* white breast; dark head and back; streaked dark band across the belly.

STATUS: Fairly common migrant and summer resident throughout the region; less common in the western parts of the region.

Highly adaptable, the Red-tailed Hawk is the most common hawk in the region. Rodents and rabbits seem to be taken most often, but this versatile hunter will also nab birds, snakes, frogs, and virtually anything else it can catch —even rattlesnakes.

Red-tailed Hawks inhabit open country with groves of large trees suitable for holding bulky nests placed 15 to 60 feet above the ground. These birds frequently use cottonwoods, elms, and oaks in the north and sycamores and walnuts further south. Occasionally, in open country without trees, the Red-tailed Hawk has been known to nest on cliffs. In the Black Hills, the birds sometimes nest on rock pinnacles.

These birds are monogamous and arrive here in the spring with their mates. Courtship displays involve soaring and swooping together and may serve to stimulate and synchronize the breeding physiology of the two birds. Both sexes help build the nest and incubate. The male feeds the female during early incubation.

Red-tailed Hawks winter throughout much of the United States and return to the same nest year after year. Because of its predatory habits, the Red-tail has suffered from misplaced persecution by people intent on protecting their small domestic animals. In reality, the hawk's primary prey are often rodents and other species considered agricultural pests.

——SIMILAR SPECIES——

Ferruginous Hawk
Buteo regalis

FIELD MARKS: 25 inches. *Light phase:* light head; **dark legs form V against light belly**; tail light and unbanded; primary feathers light and black tipped. *Dark phase:* head lighter than back; tail light and unbanded from below; mottled white and reddish above; primary feathers light and black-tipped; dark chest, underwing coverts, and legs.

STATUS: Fairly common summer resident throughout the region; more common in the west.

HOT SPOTS: Pawnee Buttes, CO; Oglala NG, NE.

These large, mild-mannered hawks frequent open habitats where they hunt from the ground, from a perch, or while soaring. Ferruginous Hawks eat a variety of

Red-tailed Hawk —Photo by Tom J. Ulrich

Ferruginous Hawks

prey, including rodents, insects, snakes, and birds, but prefer ground squirrels when available. They nest on power structures, on ledges of buttes and cliffs, in ground nests on hillsides, and on nesting structures provided for them by biologists.

Swainson's Hawk   *Buteo swainsoni*

FIELD MARKS: 21 inches. Finely barred, long tail with broad terminal band. *In flight:* often holds wings up in a shallow V like a harrier. *Dark phase:* dark head, back, primaries, chest, and belly. *Light phase:* **dark head and back; dark chest band.**

STATUS: Fairly common throughout most of the region; migrant only in the BH; common breeder in BLNP.

HOT SPOTS: Pawnee Buttes, CO; Oglala NG, NE.

Similar to the above two hawks in hunting methods and prey preference, Swainson's Hawks are relatively tame and unaggressive for a hawk. Their flimsy stick nests are built in trees or on cliffs. Winters are spent in Argentina—a round-trip of 11,000 to 17,000 miles—making them the champion travelers among the hawks of this region.

Swainson's Hawk

FALCONS

American Kestrel   *Falco sparverius*

FIELD MARKS: 9 inches. **Small size; rusty back and tail** with black bars; "mustache"; pointed wings. ***Male:*** bluish wings. ***Female:*** brown wings and tail.

STATUS: Common summer resident throughout the region and in the BH; uncommon winter resident.

The smallest and most widespread of the falcons, American Kestrels inhabit open country and hunt from a perch on a telephone wire or while hovering in the air. Kestrels feed mostly on insects but will also take mice, frogs, and small birds. In addition to open country for hunting, American Kestrels need large trees with cavities of sufficient size to hold their nests. Old woodpecker holes and crevices in cliffs or buildings are sometimes used, as are large nest boxes put out by concerned bird lovers. Nests are usually located from 8 to 30 feet above the ground.

A pair raises an average of four young. For the first three weeks the male brings food, which the female tears apart and feeds to the young. After that both parents begin bringing whole prey to the nest for the young to tear apart. Fledging occurs at about thirty days and the family group may forage together for some time after. The warning call, *"killy-killy-killy,"* is distinctive.

——SIMILAR SPECIES——

Prairie Falcon   *Falco mexicanus*

FIELD MARKS: 16 inches; medium size; pale brown above, light below. ***In flight:*** pointed wings; quick wing beats; **black "armpits."**

STATUS: Local breeder in the western part of the region; uncommon migrant throughout the same area.

HOT SPOTS: Pawnee Buttes, CO; Scotts Bluff NM, NE; Gering, NE.

Prairie Falcons inhabit dry, sagebrush-covered semidesert flats and plains. They hunt mainly ground squirrels. After spotting prey, the Prairie Falcon pursues it by a "stoop" or dive, which may reach speeds approaching 200 miles per hour. Prairie Falcons build no nest, merely laying their eggs in a "scrape" on a protected ledge on the face of a cliff. Intruders are warned off with a fierce *"kik-kik-kik."*

Peregrine Falcon   *Falco peregrinus*

FIELD MARKS: 18 inches. Dark above; light below; **dark "mustache."** ***In flight:*** medium size; lacks the dark "armpits" of the Prairie Falcon.

STATUS: Endangered species. Extremely rare breeder and uncommon migrant; in this region believed to nest only in the BH.

The widespread use of pesticides extirpated this species throughout much of its range. The Peregrine Falcon nests on tall, largely inaccessible cliffs, and hunts mainly birds—waterfowl, shorebirds, and songbirds. Capable of "stooping" at speeds exceeding 200 miles per hour, it is our fastest bird. Specialized baffles in the nostrils allow it to breathe during the stoop. A Peregrine kills its prey by overtaking it in midair and either striking it with a "fisted" foot or by grasping it with sharp talons. Efforts are being made to reintroduce it to parts of its historic range, and Peregrines have reoccupied some of their traditional nesting sites.

Male American Kestrel

Female American Kestrel

Peregrine Falcon

Prairie Falcon

RAILS, COOTS, AND CRANES
ORDER GRUIFORMES

Rails, Coots, and Cranes form a diverse group of wading birds. All have long legs, but other features, such as body size and shape, bill size, and neck length vary considerably.

Rails and Coots (Family Rallidae) are small to medium-sized birds that inhabit the emergent vegetation of marshes and lakeshores. Their compact bodies, short necks, long legs, and long toes enable them to move easily over, under, and between the reeds in pursuit of the small invertebrates and insects they feed on. Shy and retiring, they are more often heard than seen. Rails build their nests just above the surface of the water and have large clutches. The adults share the domestic duties.

Cranes (Family Gruidae) are tall, long-legged birds with long necks and heavy bodies. Cranes fly with their head extended, distinguishing them from herons. They lay two eggs per year.

Sora Rail

American Coot

Sandhill Crane courtship display

Coots

American Coot
Fulica americana

FIELD MARKS: 14 inches. Slate gray plumage; red eye; stout white bill; white under tail; yellowish green legs; head pumps forward and backward while swimming.

STATUS: Common to abundant summer resident in suitable habitat throughout the region.

Often mistaken for ducks, American Coots are usually seen on ponds or marshes with open water, as well as dense stands of cattails or reeds. Excellent swimmers, coots do not have webbed toes like the ducks but they do have lobed toes, which aid them while swimming—something they do much more than the other rails. Coots have their own peculiar way of swimming, head bobbing back and forth as they go. When disturbed, they flail their wings and run across the surface of the water for long distances before finally becoming airborne, legs dangling.

Highly territorial, "mud hens" sometimes battle over nesting space. They may protect their nesting area from intruders of all species. The floating nest made of dead stems may contain between two and twelve eggs. The young are a bright orange when they hatch, but grow rapidly, and soon become pale gray, downy, miniature versions of the adults.

Coots eat seeds, leaves, roots, insects, snails, worms, and small fish. They can dive to more than 25 feet to feed on plants. They also tip in shallow water like the puddle ducks and graze on shore. Coots are not above waiting on the surface to steal plants from feeding Canvasbacks or other diving ducks. American Coots from this region winter in the Gulf of Mexico.

American Coot

American Coot

Young American Coot

CRANES

Sandhill Crane *Grus canadensis*

FIELD MARKS: 48 inches. **Gray plumage; red crown. *In flight:* flies with neck outstretched.**

STATUS: Locally abundant spring and fall migrant throughout most of the region; isolated breeder in northern part of the region; migrant only in the BH; abundant in BLNP.

HOT SPOTS: Platte River: Grand Island to Lexington and North Platte to Sutherland, NE; Medicine Lake NWR, MT; J. Clark Salyer NWR, ND; Pocasse NWR, SD; Red Lion and Jumbo Reservoir SWAs, CO.

Stately but shy, Sandhill Cranes mate for life and, just prior to nesting in spring, perform a balletlike dance to reinforce the pair-bond. In synchronized movement the cranes leap as high as 6 to 8 feet in the air as they dip, bow, stretch, and call to each other. As they dance, the birds use their bills to toss sticks and grass.

Sandhills nest in shallow, wet meadows. Because incubation begins with the laying of the first egg, (usually) two reddish brown chicks hatch two days apart, resulting in one chick being larger than the other. The two young are carefully tended by the adults for about two months. In years with limited food supplies, the older chick may outcompete the younger sibling for food, exaggerating the size difference. In some instances, the "colts" may fight and the older chick may kill the younger chick. The colts develop slowly and may not reach sexual maturity and display the slate gray plumage of the adult until they are four years old.

Sandhill Cranes migrate to and from their wintering grounds in Texas and along the Gulf Coast of Texas and northern Mexico in large flocks, stopping at many favored resting spots in this region. In late March of each year, the 60-mile section of the Platte River in Nebraska from Grand Island to Lexington draws birdwatchers from all across North America to watch the 500,000 Sandhill Cranes that congregate there to feed and rest on their way north. This meandering section of the Platte is shallow, wide, and slow, providing ideal conditions for the Sandhill Cranes and many other species of waterfowl. The cranes forage in nearby meadows for small insects, amphibians, rodents, grain, seeds, and roots, but invariably return to water to roost for the night. The flights to and from the nighttime roosting areas on the river are spectacular.

Sandhill Crane

Whooping Crane *Grus americana*

FIELD MARKS: 60 inches. *Adult:* tall; white plumage; black wingtips; long bill; black cap with red crown and malar. *Juvenile:* light brown above, white below.

STATUS: Endangered species. Rare migrant through the region; accidental in the BH; occasional in BLNP.

HOT SPOTS: Occasional almost everywhere but has been seen at the following: Medicine Lake NWR, MT; Platte River, NE; Valentine NWR, NE; Sand Lake NWR, SD; Audubon NWR, ND.

Whooping Cranes once nested only in Wood Buffalo State Park, Northwest Territories, Canada. Nearly extirpated in the early 1900s, the total population consisted of just fifteen individuals in 1914. Careful conservation efforts have brought the population back to just over 216 individuals as of February 2006. Ongoing attempts to establish breeding populations in other areas have met with limited success. A resident breeding population in Florida numbering 66 birds and a migratory flock in Wisconsin—45 birds who are led to wintering areas in Florida by ultralight plane—have resulted in a total population of 453 Whooping Cranes (including captive birds) alive as of March 2005.

Whooping Crane —Photo by Tom J. Ulrich

SHOREBIRDS, GULLS, AND TERNS
ORDER CHARADRIIFORMES

Shorebirds, Gulls, and Terns are small to medium-sized birds, most of whom, as their name implies, patrol the shorelines of lakes, ponds, rivers, and marshes for aquatic insects and other small invertebrates. While most have long legs for feeding in up to several inches of water without getting wet, some have webbed feet that enable them to feed while swimming. A few prefer uplands to the water's edge. Long, pointed wings facilitate their migratory lifestyle. This group includes several of the world's greatest travelers—they nest in Canada and Alaska and fly as far south as Central America to spend the winters. The sexes are similarly outfitted in rather cryptic shades of white, gray, and brown.

Plovers (Family Charadriidae) are small to medium-sized shorebirds with relatively short bills and shorter necks than the rest of the shorebirds. Their heads are often distinctively marked. Plovers nest directly on the ground and usually lay four eggs.

American Golden Plover

Stilts and Avocets (Family Recurvirostridae) are medium to large shorebirds whose Latin name describes their long, thin, upturned or straight bills. As their exceptionally long legs might suggest, they feed on insects and small aquatic invertebrates in deeper water than most other shorebirds.

American Avocet

Sandpipers (Family Scolopacidae) are a large and diverse group of wading and upland birds mostly clothed in dull gray, buff, or brown plumage. Variations in wing, rump or tail markings identify the different species. Their legs and bills are long and slender, ideal for probing soft mud or shallow water for small invertebrates. Except for the phalaropes, the sexes are virtually identical.

Wilson's Phalarope

Sandpipers breed on the barren grounds and muskegs of the Arctic and subarctic, and winter in South America.

Gulls and Terns (Family Laridae) are colonial nesters with webbed feet and long, pointed wings, and are graceful and adept in flight.

Gulls (Subfamily Larinae) have heavy bills that hook at the tip, a feature that enables them to grasp a wide variety of prey. Unlike terns, gulls often float on the water. Gulls traditionally fed on dead or dying fish or patrolled the shorelines for grasshoppers and crickets, but soon expanded their foraging behavior to take advantage of easy food provided by humans. The sexes are similar.

Ring-billed Gulls

Terns (Subfamily Sterninae), in contrast to the heavy-bodied gulls, have thin, pointed bills, narrow wings, and forked tails—features that give them a more delicate and graceful appearance. They fly quickly and lightly over the water in search of small fish. They can frequently be seen hovering over the water and then plunging headfirst to capture small fish. They may also pick bits of food from the surface of the water or hawk insects out of the air. Terns rarely light on the water, preferring instead to rest on shore or on floating debris. They lay two or three eggs.

Forster's Tern landing on nest

PLOVERS

Killdeer
Charadrius vociferus

FIELD MARKS: 10 inches. Brown back; white underneath; **double black breast band**; rusty rump and longish tail.

STATUS: Common to abundant summer resident throughout the region.

Nesting Killdeer occupy a wide variety of open habitats—shorelines, pastures, farm fields, golf courses, ball fields, roadsides, and lawns—often far from water. Killdeer pair up after their arrival on the nesting areas. Once paired, they vigorously defend the area around the nest. Sometime in May they lay their four eggs directly on bare ground in a gravelly, stony, or sandy area. The adults share the 25-day incubation duties.

Unlike some birds, who sit tight on the nest almost until they are stepped on, the Killdeer slips off the nest as the intruder approaches. If the intruder wanders too close, the adult feigns a broken wing to draw the danger away from the nest. Almost immediately after hatching, the young leave the nest and begin pecking at food particles. If danger is perceived to threaten the chicks, the adults employ the same feigned injury strategy. Meanwhile, the young scatter and freeze until the danger has passed.

Before and after nesting, Killdeer can be found more frequently along shorelines. Wherever they are foraging, they feed mainly on insects they pick from the surface of the ground. Their call is a distinctive *"killdeer."*

——SIMILAR SPECIES——

Semipalmated Plover
Charadrius semipalmatus

FIELD MARKS: 6 inches. **Stubby orange bill with black tip;** distinctive marked head with white forehead, black stripe in front of and below the eyes, and gray brown crown; **single, narrow, black breast band;** gray-brown back and wings, **yellow-orange legs.**

STATUS: Fairly common spring and fall migrant throughout the region; rare in the BH; uncommon in BLNP.

In spring and fall, large flocks of Semipalmated Plovers traverse the region as they travel between their wintering areas along the Gulf Coast and their nesting grounds in Alaska and northern Canada. They can be seen resting and feeding on plowed fields, area beaches, and mudflats. They rarely wade in the water, preferring to race about on the damp sand or flats, where they pick bits of food off the surface.

Piping Plover
Charadrius melodus

FIELD MARKS: 5 inches. Pale back, yellow legs and feet; single (sometimes incomplete) breast band; yellow bill with dark tip.

STATUS: Endangered species. Uncommon migrant; rare but locally common resident along the Missouri River and its western tributaries; breeds locally throughout central ND; not found in the BH or BLNP.

HOT SPOTS: Long Lake and Lake Ilo NWRs, ND; Medicine Lake NWR and Fort Peck Reservoir, MT.

Like many threatened birds, nesting habitat appears to be the factor limiting population levels. Piping Plovers nest on open sand and gravel beaches or sparsely vegetated shorelines of shallow lakes—especially those with salt-encrusted gravel, sand, or pebbly mud. These habitats are threatened by the fluctuating water levels associated with the sporadic release of water from dams along the Missouri River system.

Killdeer

Semipalmated Plover
—Photo by Tom J. Ulrich

Piping Plover
—Photo by Tom J. Ulrich

STILTS AND AVOCETS

American Avocet
Recurvirostra americana

FIELD MARKS: 18 inches. **Light brown head, neck, and breast;** black wings with white bars; white below; **long, black, upturned bill;** long, thin, blue gray legs; webbed toes. Sexes differ only in that the female has a more sharply upturned bill.

STATUS: Fairly common summer resident in appropriate alkaline habitats throughout the region; less common in the western part of the region; not found in the BH; uncommon in BLNP.

One of the most striking shorebirds, American Avocets prefer more alkaline ponds, where they frequent the shallows, searching for food by sweeping their bills from side to side. The sweeping action stirs the bottom mud, exposing small aquatic animals and insects, which the birds promptly eat. In deeper water, they may tip up somewhat like a dabbling duck. Webbed feet enable them to swim when the occasion arises.

Avocets nest on expansive flats, shorelines, or islands with little or no vegetation. The female lays three or four olive, blotched eggs either in a shallow depression in the sand or on a small platform of grass near the water. Nest location makes the nest highly susceptible to rising water levels, whether the result of higher than normal levels of precipitation or as a result of human activity associated with impoundments and irrigation.

Incubation is about twenty-five days and both sexes participate, with the male spending comparatively more time on the nest than the female. Soon after hatching, the young leave the nest and follow the adults to the water. Both parents tend the young, but the young feed themselves. If the family is disturbed, the young scurry for cover while the adults use the broken-wing ploy to distract the intruder.

The call is a loud *"wheet, wheet."*

——SIMILAR SPECIES——

Black-necked Stilt
Himantopus mexicanus

FIELD MARKS: 14 inches. Tall, slim; **black above; white below;** straight black bill; **long, slender red legs.**

STATUS: Casual visitor; more common south and west of this region.

Appropriately named, the Black-necked Stilt frequents the muddy or grassy shorelines of shallow freshwater marshes. It walks gracefully, but its legs are so long that it must bend at the "knee" (actually the ankle joint on a bird) to pick up insects from the ground. However, these "stilts" are no handicap when the bird feeds as it often does—by actively wading through the water, daintily picking insects from the water's surface or from aquatic vegetation.

Call is a loud *"kek-kek-kek."*

American Avocet with chick

Black-necked Stilts

SANDPIPERS

Greater Yellowlegs
Tringa melanoleuca

FIELD MARKS: 14 inches. Mottled grayish brown upperparts; **long, slim, slightly upturned bill;** lightly streaked or barred breast and belly; **long, yellow legs; 3- to 5-note whistle; mostly white tail and rump.**

STATUS: Common spring and fall migrant throughout the region; rare in the BH; uncommon in BLNP.

Greater Yellowlegs that migrate through this region nest on the tundra and muskeg of north-central Canada and Alaska and winter along the Gulf Coast. While migrating through this area, they stop to rest and feed in shallow water bordered by mudflats. They rush about, catching small fish and aquatic invertebrates with rapid sweeps of their bills or by pecking food from the surface. Usually seen alone or with loose groups of fewer than ten birds. Greater Yellowlegs take flight readily when disturbed and fly with their long legs extended well beyond their tails, while uttering a *"deew deew deew"* call.

——SIMILAR SPECIES——

Lesser Yellowlegs
Tringa flavipes

FIELD MARKS: 10 inches. Plain, gray brown plumage; **bright yellow legs;** long, slim bill; **1- to 3-note whistle.**

STATUS: Abundant spring and fall migrant throughout the region; rare in the BH; common in BLNP.

Smaller, tamer, and quieter than its look-alike, the Greater Yellowlegs, the Lesser Yellowlegs is most often seen probing for food in the mud along the edges of marshes and slow rivers. A common sight in spring and fall throughout the region, Lesser Yellowlegs may also be seen feeding by skimming invertebrates from the surface of the water or from the ground. Very active feeders, they often chase through the water in pursuit of moving prey. The Lesser Yellowlegs does not feed by sweeping its bill as the Greater Yellowlegs does. When disturbed, it often bobs its head just before taking flight and utters a *"kleet kleet"* call as it departs.

Willet
Catoptrophorus semipalmatus

FIELD MARKS: 15 inches. Plain, grayish brown plumage; bluish legs; partially webbed feet; bill thicker than yellowlegs. *In flight:* **black-and-white wing pattern is diagnostic.**

STATUS: Fairly common spring and fall migrant throughout the area; fairly common breeder from north-central NE north through SD and ND; absent from higher elevations in the BH and BLNP.

Willets probe prairie marshes, seasonal ponds, and ephemeral streams for mollusks, crayfish, small fish, and insects. They occasionally pick invertebrates off the surface of the water. They nest in sloughs and along alkaline flats. Look for them in the company of avocets.

Greater Yellowlegs

Lesser Yellowlegs

Willet

Long-billed Curlew
Numenius americanus

FIELD MARKS: 24 inches. Brown plumage; large; **extremely long, decurved bill;** cinnamon wing linings.

STATUS: Fairly common summer resident in southwestern ND, western SD, and northwestern NE, and west through MT and WY; not found in the BH.

Long-billed Curlews feed by probing in the mud with their long bills or dunking their heads underwater in search of insects, insect larvae, mollusks, crustaceans, and small amphibians. While they often frequent short-grass prairies and other dry habitats far from water, they prefer to nest in scattered colonies in damp, grassy hollows near moist meadows. The nest consists of a slight depression in the ground lined with forbs and grasses. Nesting peaks in May and June. The male shares incubation duties for the four eggs with the slightly larger female, and also helps tend the young. While raising their young on the grasslands, curlews feed mostly on insects. Call is a distinctive, drawn out *"cur-lee-w-w."*

By early August, all have left the area. During winter, they frequent tidal flats and saltwater beaches.

————SIMILAR SPECIES————

Marbled Godwit
Limosa fedoa

FIELD MARKS: 18 inches. Dark, mottled above; cinnamon buff with barring below; cinnamon wing linings; **long, orange, upturned bill with black tip; dark legs.**

STATUS: Fairly common migrant throughout the region; uncommon summer resident in ND and northeast SD; rare migrant in the BH; not reported in BLNP.

Second in size only to the Long-billed Curlew, Marbled Godwits live on a diet of insects, worms, mollusks, and crustaceans. They often gather in small flocks and feed by rapidly thrusting their bills into the soft ground of mudflats. Birders will easily identify this bird by its call because it calls its own name: *"god-wit."*

Upland Sandpiper
Bartramia longicauda

FIELD MARKS: 10 inches. Long neck, small head, short bill; yellow legs; flies stiffly and holds wings erect for short time after landing.

STATUS: Common summer resident throughout the region; local in the BH; common in BLNP.

Although their head and bill differ radically from those of the Long-billed Curlew, Upland Sandpipers closely resemble curlews in their habits, voice, and overall body structure. They can often be seen perched on fence posts or power poles in upland habitats of native grasslands. They spend very little time in wetlands. While feeding, Upland Sandpipers run, stop, and run again, while searching for insects, invertebrates, and available grass and weed seeds. The future well-being of the species depends on the abundance of native prairie habitats for nesting. Upland Sandpipers spend their winters in eastern South America, making them the shorebird with the longest migration route among those breeding in the region.

Long-billed Curlew

Marbled Godwit

Upland Sandpiper

Wilson's Snipe *Gallinago delicata*

FIELD MARKS: 11 inches. **Extremely long bill; very stocky body;** short legs; boldly striped brown back and chest, white belly.

STATUS: Common spring and fall migrant; breeding resident in ND and northern SD, and in MT and WY; breeder in the BH; uncommon breeder in BLNP.

Most commonly seen perched on a roadside fence post near soggy meadows, Wilson's Snipe is an easy bird to recognize with its extremely long bill. Solitary and usually secretive except while perching, snipe frequent marshes and other shallow water in areas of mucky organic soils and sparse vegetation.

Like other shorebirds, the snipe uses its bill to probe for invertebrates in the moist ground. When the sensitive tip encounters food—in the form of an insect, insect larvae, or earthworm—the bird uses the bill's prehensile tip to quickly grasp the morsel and pull it to the surface.

Males arrive on the nesting grounds first. Once there they establish territories and attract females with "winnowing" flights. These flight displays, performed either by day or night, are often heard before the bird is seen. Sometimes, even though the flight can be heard, the bird is so high in the sky that it defies detection. The male snipe begins the display by climbing high in the sky. From there, he performs a sudden, deep, high-speed dive that produces a low, hollow, pulsing, whistling/wavering sound as air rushes through the bird's widespread outer tail feathers: "*huhuhuhuhuhuhuhuhuhuhuh.*"

Females may mate with more than one male but eventually associate with a single male while building a nest in his territory. The female chooses a nest site in a boggy area, often near a beaver pond, on a small hummock hidden in tall grass. She carefully weaves dried vegetation from the previous year into a canopy that hides the nest. As a final touch, she lines the nest with fine grasses.

The female lays the four eggs in late May or early June and then incubates them without the help of the male. While the female incubates the eggs, the male may court other females. The pair-bond disappears completely when the young hatch and the male takes the first couple of young and tends them by himself, leaving the remaining chicks for the female to tend.

When threatened, the snipe relies on its protective coloring for security, flushing only at the last instant and soon dropping back into tall vegetation. When disturbed, the snipe often utters a "*TIKa TIKa TIKa*" call or a "*Wheat-wheat-wheat*" call.

Wilson's Snipe

Wilson's Snipe

GULLS

Ring-billed Gull
Larus delawarensis

FIELD MARKS: 18 inches. White plumage; gray wings; **black ring around bill; yellowish legs and feet.** Sexes are similar.

STATUS: Local breeding resident in northern and northeastern ND and eastern SD; common migrant and uncommon to occasional winter resident throughout the region.

HOT SPOTS: Lakes McConaughy and Ogallala, NE.

The most common gull in the region, the Ring-billed Gull has adapted and expanded its range, moving into residential areas as its traditional habitat has shrunk. Gulls frequent shorelines and may be seen floating on the water, where their webbed feet allow them to move about easily. In natural habitats, gulls feed on dead or dying fish and patrol shorelines for grasshoppers and crickets. However, as humans have continued to alter the natural habitats, these adaptable birds have learned to take advantage of virtually any easy food provided by humans. Look for gulls in freshly plowed or flooded fields, city parks, sanitary landfills, or even supermarket and restaurant parking lots. They also act as predators by preying on the eggs and young of other birds.

Ring-billed Gulls nest in colonies on sparsely vegetated islands. The nest is a small mound placed directly on the ground. The two or three eggs are incubated by both parents and hatch in about three weeks. The young are semiprecocial and remain at the nest for about two weeks. Both parents guard and feed the young until they fledge at five weeks.

Gulls go through several variations in plumage coloration over their first four years of life. You can find descriptions of these plumages in some of the more advanced guidebooks given in the "Suggested References" section.

Winters are spent along the Pacific coast; landfills and rivers (particularly below dams) in the interior also support wintering flocks.

——SIMILAR SPECIES——

Franklin's Gull
Larus pipixcan

FIELD MARKS: 15 inches. Black head; red bill; partial broad white eye ring; gray back and wings; white neck and underparts.

STATUS: Regular breeder in eastern two-thirds of ND and northeastern SD; migrant elsewhere in the region, including the BH and BLNP.

HOT SPOTS: Long Lake and Souris Loop NWRs, ND; Sand Lake and Waubay NWRs, SD.

Franklin's Gulls build their floating nests in scattered colonies. Nests of adjacent pairs are closer together in heavy vegetation where visibility is limited and further apart in sparse vegetation where visibility is better. Unlike many other gulls, Franklin's Gulls do not eat eggs or chicks of other Franklin's Gulls. The chicks do not learn to recognize their own parents until they are at least two weeks old, and the parents apparently sometimes adopt young chicks from nearby nests. Franklin's Gulls are the only gulls that go through two complete molts each year, resulting in a clean, fresh look year-round.

Ring-billed Gulls

Franklin's Gull

TERNS

Forster's Tern
Sterna forsteri

FIELD MARKS: 13 inches. Pale gray above, white below; **black crown and nape;** orange bill; **tail has white outer edges;** white wing tips.

STATUS: Common summer resident in the east and Lacreek NWR, SD; uncommon visitor in the west, including the BH and BLNP.

Forster's Terns are the most common black-capped tern in the region. They frequent shallow marshes with emergent vegetation and islands for nesting. Colonial nesters, Forster's terns have highly stereotyped and elaborate breeding rituals that involve sky-pointing, bill-drooping, wing-drooping, billing, and calling. Entire colonies seem to synchronize their breeding, with all the young hatching within a relatively short period of time. Colonies may return to the same islands for nesting year after year. After a summer of raising their young, they move south and winter along the Gulf Coast.

——SIMILAR SPECIES——

Black Tern
Chlidonias niger

FIELD MARKS: 10 inches. **All-black plumage;** gray wings; shallowly forked tail.

STATUS: Abundant migrant and common summer resident in the east; uncommon in the west and in the BH and BLNP.

Tame and almost friendly birds, Black Terns prefer marshes with abundant emergent vegetation. Nests are a shallow cup of reeds on a muskrat house or a low tussock or a frail platform among the reeds. More insectivorous than the other terns, Black Terns hawk insects from the air or skim them from the surface of the water.

Least Tern
Sterna antillarum

FIELD MARKS: 9 inches. Black cap; **white forehead; yellow bill;** gray back; white below; two dark primaries.

STATUS: Endangered species. Ranges along both coasts and along large river systems; local breeder along the Missouri River system to central ND; not found in the BH or in BLNP.

HOT SPOTS: DeSoto and Valentine NWRs, NE.

In this region, Least Terns nest only on river sandbars and islands exposed by dropping water levels along the Mississippi and Missouri river systems. With the building of the dams on the Missouri River, much of their nesting habitat disappeared under reservoirs. Currently on the rare and endangered list, Least Terns depend at least to some degree on the management of the water levels and the timing and volume of the release of water from those dams.

Forster's Tern

Black Tern —Photo by Tom J. Ulrich

Least Tern —Photo by Tom J. Ulrich

PIGEONS AND DOVES
ORDER COLUMBIFORMES

Pigeons and Doves (Family Columbidae) are ground-feeding birds with small heads, short legs, long pointed wings, and fan-shaped or pointed tails. They bob their heads when they walk. Pigeons (generally larger than doves) and doves eat seeds, grains, nuts, and berries. Unlike most birds, they are able to suck water up into their throats and swallow without raising their heads. They need a plentiful supply of water daily to help soften the dry hard seeds they eat.

Pigeons and doves lay one or two eggs in a clutch (but may raise up to four broods each year) and share the incubation—the female incubates during the day and the male at night. The young, or squabs, hatch naked and totally helpless. Pigeons and doves feed their squabs "pigeon milk"—a regurgitated cottage cheese-like mixture of skin sloughed from the lining of the crop and partially digested seeds.

Mourning Dove   *Zenaida macroura*

FIELD MARKS: 12 inches. Small; grayish brown plumage; **long, pointed tail; wings whistle in flight.**

STATUS: Abundant breeder throughout the region in virtually all habitats.

Although they are very social for most of the year, Mourning Doves become highly territorial during the nesting season. Pair-bonds are formed in the winter flocks, with the more dominant males pairing with the higher-ranking females. Mourning Doves are monogamous and the males aggressively defend territories. During the breeding season, the male has a small iridescent spot on his neck, and his blue eye ring and red legs intensify in color.

Mourning doves build their nest (a flimsy, haphazard pile of sticks) either on the ground or in a tree, where strong winds sometimes destroy it. Mourning Doves are fairly prolific breeders because they make up for their small clutches by raising multiple broods. In this region, four broods in a nesting season are believed to be the maximum, but in Texas, one hardworking pair was observed raising six broods in a single nesting season, using three nests in the process. The young fledge in about two weeks. By the time the young in the first brood reach fledging, the parents already have another clutch started in a new nest.

The Mourning Dove lives and breeds in virtually all habitats in the region, making it a familiar sight to almost everyone. Most Mourning Doves move south in fall, but some winter here.

Mourning Dove

Rock Pigeon

Columba livia

FIELD MARKS: 13 inches. Large, stout body; **white rump**; plumage color varies widely.

STATUS: Common resident in urban and rural settings throughout the region; may nest on cliffs in the BH; common breeder in BLNP.

The wild form of the domestic pigeon, the Rock Pigeon was introduced into North America by Europeans in the early 1600s. Selective breeding of domestic stock has produced diverse plumages: black, brown, white, and various combinations of these colors. Rock Pigeons may raise several broods each year. They are most common around buildings or other human-made structures, but also use cliffs and crevices for nesting.

Rock Pigeon

OWLS
ORDER STRIGIFORMES

Owls are one of the most easily recognized groups of birds. These primarily nocturnal raptors are equipped with large eyes set forward on their heads to provide binocular vision, which is invaluable in locating and focusing on fast-moving prey. Extremely sensitive ears, unequal in size and located behind facial discs that apparently help focus the sound, can pinpoint prey in total darkness. Flight feathers, with their soft leading edges, allow almost noiseless flight.

Owls swallow small prey whole but tear larger prey into bite-sized pieces with their powerful talons and strong hooked beaks. Indigestible bones, fur, and feathers are regurgitated in the form of "owl pellets."

The females are generally larger than the males and begin incubating their eggs immediately after laying the first egg, allowing the young to hatch at intervals. The oldest, and therefore the largest, chick insists on being fed first. Only when he is satiated does the next one get to eat. In lean years, the youngest and weakest may not survive, but this method maximizes the chance that at least some of the young will survive to carry on the species. Each species of owl has a distinctive call and most are easily attracted in spring by imitating or playing recordings of their calls.

Barn Owls (Family Tytonidae) have a heart-shaped facial disc and a noticeably long rostrum (nose and beak). They have no ear tufts.

Typical Owls (Family Strigidae) have a rounder facial disc and a relatively short rostrum (nose and beak). Many, but not all, have ear tufts.

Great Horned Owl

Long-eared Owl

Northern Saw-whet Owl

BARN OWLS

Barn Owl
Tyto alba

FIELD MARKS: 14 inches. Large, white, **heart-shaped facial disc;** dark eyes; light golden brown above with small black spots, white below with small black spots; long legs.

STATUS: Local summer resident in open country throughout the southern part of the region; accidental in MT, ND, and northern SD; not found in the BH, rare in BLNP.

HOT SPOTS: Medicine Creek WMA, Cambridge, NE; Fort Robinson SP, Crawford, NE.

Barn Owls feed primarily on small mammals such as mice, voles, and shrews. Because of their habit of taking advantage of barns to provide shelter during nesting, Barn Owls are often closely associated with man. In this region, they also use chalk cliffs, shale bluffs, and riverbanks, as well as secluded corners of other man-made structures such as silos, church steeples, or other buildings.

Believed to pair for life, the mates engage in greeting behaviors which stimulate mutual prey-presentation and eventually, copulation. The pair does not build a nest; instead, the female simply deposits her eggs on whatever substrate happens to cover her chosen nest site. She begins incubating with the first egg but may lay from three to six more pure white, elliptical eggs.

The female does all the incubation, although the male sometimes brings her food at the nest. After about thirty days, the young begin hatching at intervals of two to three days. The male continues to bring food, which the female tears apart and feeds to the young. The chicks fledge at eight weeks but continue to be fed by adults for about another month, when they leave the home territory to fend for themselves. In years of plentiful prey, Barn Owls may begin a second breeding cycle and raise another brood.

When approached at its nest, a Barn Owl will often lower its head and move it from side to side, which may be an attempt to get a better look at the intruder or simply a nervous response to the disturbance.

——SIMILAR SPECIES——

Snowy Owl
Bubo scandiacus

FIELD MARKS: 24 inches. Large; yellow eyes; no ear tufts; **white plumage** with small black spots or bars.

STATUS: Irregular winter visitor throughout the region; not found in the BH; occasional in BLNP.

Snowy owls nest and raise their young on the open tundra of northern Alaska and northern Canada. In some years, prompted by a short supply of rodents, they move south, occasionally reaching this region, where they soon attract the attention of birders.

Barn Owl —Photo by Alan G. Nelson

Snowy Owl

Typical Owls

Great Horned Owl
Bubo virginianus

FIELD MARKS: 22 inches. Large; **ear tufts;** horizontal bars on belly. *Voice:* a deep, low ***who-whoowhoo-whooo***.

STATUS: Common permanent resident throughout the region, including the BH and BLNP.

The Great Horned Owl is the most common owl in the region and found in all types of woodlands. This highly efficient predator prefers rabbits but takes a wide variety of birds, mammals, and reptiles. Remains of dogs, cats, skunks, porcupines, rattlesnakes, and even Peregrine Falcons have been found in their castings.

When the February breeding season rolls around, pairs of Great Horned Owls establish their territories and keep in contact with each other by using their familiar *"who-whoowhoo-whooo"* calls. The pair takes possession of an old hawk or heron nest, a tree hollow, an appropriate ledge or crevice, or even an undisturbed corner of a building, and the female lays two to four eggs. Great Horned Owls are almost fearless when defending their young, and may even attack humans who venture too close.

------SIMILAR SPECIES------

Eastern Screech-Owl
Megascops asio

FIELD MARKS: 9 inches. Small; **yellow eyes; ear tufts;** grayish plumage. *Voice:* a quavering whistle.

STATUS: Fairly common resident throughout the wooded habitats in the region, including the BH; uncommon in BLNP.

A pint-sized version of the Great Horned Owl, the Eastern Screech-Owl is also very common in this region (although less common toward the western part of the region). Screech-Owls occupy many habitat types—suburbs, orchards, farms, river bottoms, and aspen and ponderosa pine forests.

They take mice from the meadow and large insects from the air or from foliage, as well as bats, crayfish, fish, reptiles, frogs, worms, and birds. An early study documented that over a 45-day period, adults fed their young seventy-seven birds of eighteen different species, including sparrows, warblers, phoebes, and tanagers. A wide variety of insects, mammals, salamanders, crayfish, and other prey were also brought to the young.

Screech-Owls nest in tree cavities, laying four or five eggs in April.

Great Horned Owl

Fledgling Great Horned Owl

Eastern Screech-Owl.
— © Brian E. Small/www.briansmallphoto.com

Short-eared Owl
Asio flammeus

FIELD MARKS: 15 inches. Medium size; appears earless; **light belly with vertical stripes.** *In flight:* black "wrist" marks; **flies with a buoyant lilt.** *Voice:* a raspy bark.

STATUS: Uncommon to fairly common resident in open habitats throughout the region; absent from the BH; uncommon in BLNP.

An owl of open country, the Short-eared Owl can often be seen in broad daylight, perched on fence posts or power poles or drifting low over the grasslands, searching for small rodents. Powered by slow, relaxed wing strokes, the Short-eared Owl flies with a characteristic erratic bounce.

In spring, pairs can be seen performing their acrobatic courtship flights. High over the prairies, the pair swoop, dive, and perform wing-claps and somersaults, accompanied by their characteristic quavering, chattering call.

The nest is built on the ground in a slight depression and lined with a few grasses or feathers to hold the four to nine white eggs. The male brings food to the female during incubation and after the young have hatched. Incubation takes about thirty-two days. The young begin venturing away from the nest at about two weeks and begin catching small prey at about six weeks. The adults continue to feed the young until well after they are flying. Intruders venturing too close to the nest or to the young are lured away by the adults using the crippled-bird display.

Because the diet of these birds is about 90 percent rodents, the Short-eared Owl can be very beneficial to humans from an economic standpoint. The main concern for this species is loss of habitat to agriculture.

————SIMILAR SPECIES————

Burrowing Owl
Athene cunicularia

FIELD MARKS: 9 inches. Small; **long, nearly bare legs;** no ear tufts; nests in burrow. *Voice:* soft *coo-coooo* or a cackling alarm call.

STATUS: Locally common summer resident in dry, open areas of the region; rare in the BH; common in BLNP.

HOT SPOTS: Lacreek NWR, SD.

While most owls nest in trees, Burrowing Owls, as their name implies, nest in burrows in the ground. Prairie dog holes or burrows confiscated from other rodents, badgers, or even tortoises are modified into suitable quarters for raising young. In some cases, in areas with suitable soils, the birds may excavate their own burrow. The burrow usually consists of a 4- to 9-foot tunnel ending in a nest cavity, which is usually lined with vegetation or dried manure. The entrance to the tunnel is also often marked with manure, presumably to disguise the scent from predators.

Burrowing Owls are largely diurnal and feed on insects, small reptiles, and small mammals. When disturbed, they bob and bow before either flying a short distance away or scurrying into their burrow. Like most other owls, their success in raising young each year depends on the availability of prey. When prey is plentiful, Burrowing Owls may raise five to seven youngsters. In lean years, fewer young survive.

Because of their dependence on abandoned burrows for nesting, the numbers of Burrowing Owls have declined along with prairie dog populations.

Short-eared Owl
Inset: *Burrowing Owl*

NIGHTHAWKS
ORDER CAPRIMULGIFORMES

Nighthawks (Family Caprimulgidae) feed in flight by scooping insects out of midair. Huge scooplike mouths surrounded by long whiskers help funnel insects into their beaks. Short, weak legs barely allow them to waddle around on the ground. They occasionally perch in trees, but when they do, they perch lengthwise on the branches rather than crosswise like most birds.

Common Nighthawk   *Chordeiles minor*

FIELD MARKS: 8 inches. Mottled brown and gray plumage; tiny beak. *Male:* **white tail band and white throat;** *Female:* **lacks white tail band and has buffy throat.** *In flight:* long, pointed wings; **white bar on lower wing;** square or slightly notched tail.

STATUS: Common to abundant resident throughout the region, including the BH and BLNP.

A first glance at their short, weak legs and tiny beaks might leave an observer with the impression that Common Nighthawks are ill-equipped for survival. However, long, pointed wings that make them very capable and nimble in flight, coupled with capacious mouths, make them ideally suited to feed by scooping insects out of midair. Careful observers throughout most of the region, particularly around some cities and towns, may see these birds flying around in the early morning or just at dusk. They also feed at night and sometimes during cloudy days. While feeding, they fly erratically, as they dodge and turn in pursuit of a wide variety of flying insects. This batlike feeding behavior has resulted in the nickname "bullbat."

One study in Maine discovered a nighthawk whose stomach contained 2,175 ants and a study in Massachusetts found one with over 500 mosquitoes. Common nighthawks not only feed in flight, they also drink while in flight, scooping up water by flying low and skimming the surface with their bills.

These birds arrive on their nesting grounds on the Great Plains toward the end of May, relatively late compared to most other migratory birds. The males soon begin their displays, consisting of a variety of vocal and aerial acrobatics. These include a *"peent"* call and steep dives (usually directly over the selected nest site) that end with a swoop at the bottom of the flight and a simultaneous "woof" or muffled boom produced by the rushing air causing his primaries to vibrate.

Common Nighthawks do not build a nest; the female simply lays her two eggs on the bare ground in an exposed location. Typically an open, gravelly location is chosen, which could range from a graveled roof in the city, to dry badlands, to burned-over tracts left by forest fires. All of these sites are exposed to the sun and get very hot. Nighthawks combat the heat with "gular fluttering," fluttering the skin of the throat, causing air movement in and out of the open mouth.

Common Nighthawk

Common Nighthawk with chick, nineteen days old

SWIFTS AND HUMMINGBIRDS
ORDER APODIFORMES

Hummingbirds (Family Trochilidae). Apodiformes literally means "without feet." The members of this order do have feet, albeit tiny and weak, but they are masters of flight.

Hummingbirds are the smallest North American birds and expend the greatest output of energy per unit of weight of any known animal, with the exception of insects in flight. To keep up with those energy demands, hummers sip nectar from flowers for calories and eat small insects and spiders for protein. With their long, thin bills and tubelike tongues they reach deep into tubular flowers to obtain nectar. To move efficiently from flower to flower requires remarkable powers of flight and hummers can do it all—fly forward, fly backward, fly straight up, fly straight down, hover, pivot, and even perform backward somersaults. Among the most brightly colored of the birds, they wear dazzling iridescent colors on their backs, and the males sport distinctive, brightly colored, iridescent throat patches called gorgets. Different species can be identified by the pattern of their courtship flight.

Swifts (Family Apodidae) are, like their relatives the hummingbirds, built for speed. Swifts have torpedo-shaped bodies and flat, narrow, swept-back wings. In flight, they resemble swallows, but the swift's wings beat in a more hurried tempo. Creatures of the air, they eat, drink, and even breed on the wing.

Ruby-throated Hummingbird *Archilochus colubris*

FIELD MARKS: 3 3/4 inches. Tail projects beyond wingtips when perched. *Male:* **black chin, red throat;** greenish back. *Female:* green back; white underparts.

STATUS: Breeds in the eastern part of ND, SD, and NE; not found in the BH.

Ruby-throated Hummingbirds are the only hummingbirds that normally breed east of the Great Plains. The western edge of their breeding range extends into a variety of wooded habitats across the eastern edge of this region.

The female builds a half-dollar-sized nest on a horizontal branch, protected from above by an overhanging branch. The nest consists of small plant materials and spiderwebs, covered on the outside with lichens, and lined with plant down. The two pea-sized eggs are incubated by the female and hatch in about 16 days. The female feeds the young a combination of nectar and insects, which she transfers to them by thrusting her swordlike bill deep into their throats. By the time the young are ten days old, they are nearly as large as the female; they fledge at about twenty-one days.

Male Ruby-throated Hummingbird —Photo by Tom J. Ulrich

To conserve energy, Ruby-throated Hummingbirds become torpid at night. Torpor is a state in which the body temperature drops to that of the surrounding air, and both the heart rate and respiration decrease dramatically. When nighttime temperatures drop below 60 degrees, the birds may save as much as 98 percent of the energy they would otherwise use to maintain their normal body temperature.

The Ruby-throated Hummingbird can be identified by the deep, U- or cup-shaped pattern of its courtship flight.

——SIMILAR SPECIES——

Calliope Hummingbird *Stellula calliope*

FIELD MARKS: 3 1/4 inches. *Male:* striped scarlet purple gorget; greenish back; small. *Female:* green back; white underparts; short tail; no rust in center of rump.

STATUS: Breeds along the western edge of the region in MT and WY; casual fall migrant in the BH; not found in BLNP.

The scientific name of this bird loosely means "beautiful little star," referring to its small size and brilliant colors. The smallest bird in North America, the Calliope Hummingbird mainly breeds to the north of this region, in western Canada. Its pendulum-like courtship flight traces a shallow U.

Male Calliope Hummingbird

KINGFISHERS
ORDER CORACIIFORMES

Kingfishers (Family Alcedinidae), as their name implies, live primarily on fish. These chunky, compact birds, with their large bills and heads, tiny feet, short tails, and short, rounded wings, are very distinctive. Their profile is made even more recognizable by the ragged, erectile crest. Kingfishers are solitary except while nesting.

Belted Kingfisher   *Ceryle alcyon*

FIELD MARKS: 13 inches. *Male:* **oversized blue head**; white neck; blue back; large, **heavy bill**; **big, unruly crest**; bluish breast band. *Female:* similar but with an **additional chestnut breast band.**

STATUS: Fairly common breeder throughout the region; rare in winter; fairly common in the BH; rare in BLNP.

The Belted Kingfisher hunts by perching on a branch or stump near or over water or by hovering, then diving headlong into the water in pursuit of fish, amphibians, crustaceans, and aquatic insects. The speed of the dive carries it completely underwater. However, it soon emerges, carrying a small, hapless creature in its bill. More than half of the diet of these birds consists of 3- to 4-inch fish.

Kingfishers nest in burrows in cut banks in sandy clay soil, usually along streams, but also along roads, borrow pits, or other similar vertical banks. The pair dig the burrows (from 5 to 15 feet long) with their bills, pushing the dirt out with their small feet. The entrance is usually located more than 5 feet from the bottom of the bank and within 3 feet of the top of the bank. The hole is 3 to 4 inches in diameter and typically slightly wider than it is high. There is usually a dead or dying tree not far away, which is used as a sentinel post.

The pair incubates the eggs in shifts. The young are nearly helpless after hatching and spend much of their time huddling together, presumably to keep warm. The voracious appetites of as many as eight chicks keeps both adults busy bringing food. In some cases, the adults may need to forage as far as 5 miles away from the nest hole to find enough food for the growing youngsters.

The young remain hidden deep in the burrow for several weeks before emerging. They are able to fly at about a month but continue to stay near the nest while they learn to fish.

The adults teach the novice fishermen by example. The adults capture a fish, beat it on a branch until it is almost dead, and then drop it back in the water for the young to retrieve. As this process is repeated again and again, the young begin to get the idea and so learn to catch their own fish. Within ten days they are ready to survive on their own and leave the area of the nest.

Belted Kingfisher —Photo by Alan G. Nelson

WOODPECKERS
ORDER PICIFORMES

Woodpeckers (Family Picidae) have thick, heavy, chisel-like bills that enable them to reach wood-boring insects and larvae hidden under tree bark or in rotting wood. They also have shock-absorbing skulls to cushion their brains so they can withstand the hammering. Strong feet and claws and stiff tail feathers help them to hold on to vertical surfaces and brace their bodies while hammering. Thus equipped, most of them forage on the trunks and large branches of trees. Some members also take insects from the bark, the air, the foliage, or the ground, and eat nuts, berries, and fruit. In spring, woodpeckers "drum" to attract mates and establish their territories.

Male Three-toed Woodpecker

Red-naped Sapsucker

Female Northern Flicker

WOODPECKERS

Red-headed Woodpecker
Melanerpes erythrocephalus

FIELD MARKS: 9 inches. **Red head**; black back; white belly; **white rump and secondaries.**

STATUS: Fairly common to uncommon summer resident throughout much of its range; uncommon in BLNP.

Red-headed Woodpeckers prefer relatively open forests, farmlands, river bottomlands, parks, backyards, and woodlots. They often perch in the open on exposed dead branches.

Although they are woodpeckers, these birds rarely bore holes in trees to locate insects to eat. Instead, they catch most of their food in flight, from the ground, or by gleaning from tree trunks and limbs.

These large, flashy woodpeckers nest in cavities located in rather isolated dead trees; more often than not, the tree or limb selected for the nest has long since lost its bark. The cavity is usually located between 10 and 50 feet above the ground and excavated by enlarging an existing crack. The entrance hole is about 2 inches in diameter but may be irregular in shape because of the preexisting crack.

As with many other birds, the males return to the nesting areas before the females. They call from the nest hole or roost to attract mates. When a female approaches the territory, the male may tap from inside the nesting cavity. If the female comes to the cavity, the male leaves so the female can inspect it. Mutual tapping at the hole seems to confirm the pair-bond.

Nesting in this region usually occurs in June and July. Both sexes take their turn sitting on the four to seven eggs during the twelve-day incubation period. Incubation is started before the entire clutch is laid so the hatching period is extended, and the youngsters may vary considerably in size. Both sexes incubate, with the male taking over those duties at night. Red-headed Woodpeckers are known to produce second broods in some areas. With the approach of winter and the disappearance of insect food, Red-headed Woodpeckers move south for the winter.

Call is a raucous *"kwrrk."*

Red-headed Woodpecker —Photo by Tom J. Ulrich

Red-naped Sapsucker   *Sphyrapicus nuchalis*

FIELD MARKS: 8 inches. ***Male:*** black with white spots above, light below; **red crown; red nape; red throat with incomplete black border.** ***Female:*** red nape; white chin; red throat.

STATUS: Uncommon summer resident in the BH; not found in the rest of the region.

Yellow-bellied Sapsucker   *Sphyrapicus varius*

FIELD MARKS: 8 inches. ***Male:*** black with white spots above, light below; **white nape** (rarely red); **red crown; red throat with complete black border.** ***Female:*** white nape and throat.

STATUS: Uncommon summer resident along eastern border of the region; migrant throughout the eastern half; accidental elsewhere in the region, including the BH and BLNP.

The ranges of these two species of closely related sapsuckers meet at the Black Hills. The main range of the Red-naped Sapsucker lies to the west, while the main range of the Yellow-bellied Sapsucker lies to the east of the Black Hills.

Sapsuckers frequent all types of woodlands but seem to prefer aspen or poplar groves, which provide the bird with both food and shelter. Sapsuckers received their name from their habit of drilling a parallel series of holes in the bark of alders, willows, and many other trees. The holes, drilled at a slightly downward angle, fill with sap. Sapsuckers return again and again to eat the sap and the insects attracted by the sweet liquid. Hummingbirds and other species of birds may also discover the sap wells and make regular visits to feed. In addition to sap and insects, sapsuckers also feed extensively on the cambium layer of inner bark.

After spending the winter further south, the males arrive back here about the end of April and soon begin drumming to establish their territories. They begin excavating new cavities and advertise to the females by a distinctive courtship flight. Excavation is completed when both sexes accept the site.

The nest holes are usually near water, either in dead trees or in live trees with rotting cores. The entrance hole often faces the water and may be anywhere from 8 to 40 feet above the ground. Sapsuckers do not usually occupy the same cavity more than once although they may excavate a new hole in the same tree as the previous year's nest hole.

Four to six white eggs are laid and incubation duties are shared between the adults. Likewise, both partners share in feeding the young. Fed a rich diet of sap and insects, the young grow quickly and leave the nest about a month after hatching.

Red-naped Sapsucker

Yellow-bellied Sapsucker —Photo by Tom J. Ulrich

Downy Woodpecker

Picoides pubescens

FIELD MARKS: 6 inches. Black-and-white plumage; **white underparts**; white back; black wings barred with white; **bill half the length of the head or less; outer tail feathers with two or more black bars.** *Male:* red patch on nape.

STATUS: Common resident throughout most of the region; uncommon in the BH and BLNP.

The Downy Woodpecker is the most common and widespread woodpecker in the eastern United States. It uses all types of wooded habitat. In summer, the Downy takes insects from the surface of branches and foliage. In winter, when food is less plentiful and insects are less active, this woodpecker spends more time chipping for its meals. Watch as it taps on a branch, moves on, taps again, and chips away at the wood when it detects a likely insect tunnel. The bird snakes its long, barbed tongue down the hole, entangles the insect or grub, withdraws it, and eats it. This bird is often a regular at suet feeders.

Year-round residents, Downy Woodpeckers begin their territorial drumming toward the end of winter. In spring, the pairs begin to search for suitable nest sites. Either one of the pair that discovers a potential site begins tapping to attract the other. When the two agree, they both take part in the excavation, although the females seem to be more active than the males. Clutches usually consist of four or five eggs. Both sexes incubate.

The eggs hatch in about twelve days. For the first week, one of the adults is with the young at all times. As the young are more able to regulate their body temperature, and at the same time require more food, the adults begin spending more time foraging. At about two weeks, the young begin to climb to the entrance hole and meet the parents there to be fed. Fledging occurs at four to five weeks and the pair-bond begins to break down. The adults spend the winter in separate roosting holes and forage independently until the rites of spring begin again.

——SIMILAR SPECIES——

Hairy Woodpecker

Picoides villosus

FIELD MARKS: 8 inches. Black-and-white plumage; white back; black wings barred with white; **bill longer than half the length of head; white outer tail feathers usually not marked.** *Male:* red patch on nape.

STATUS: Uncommon to fairly common throughout the region; common in the BH; uncommon in BLNP.

Closely resembling a larger version of the Downy, the Hairy Woodpecker requires similar habitat, but tends to use larger trees in more heavily forested areas. It feeds on the larvae of wood-boring beetles, particularly the western pine bark beetle, and feeds more on the trunk and larger vertical branches of the trees than the Downy. The Hairy Woodpecker is also shyer, and usually flies ahead of an intruder rather than simply moving upward in the tree, as the Downy often does.

Male Downy Woodpecker

Female Downy Woodpecker

Male Hairy Woodpecker

Female Hairy Woodpecker

Northern Flicker

Colaptes auratus

FIELD MARKS: 12 inches. Two color morphs—the eastern "yellow-shafted" and the western "red-shafted."

Yellow-shafted: Brown head and neck with gray cap, red crescent on nape, and gray hind neck; **grayish brown back and belly** with black breast patch and black spots. *In flight:* **yellow flash** to underside of wings. *Male:* black mustache. *Female:* no mustache.

Red-shafted: Gray head and neck with tan forehead; **grayish brown back and belly** with black breast patch and black spots. *In flight:* **salmon flash** to underside of wings. *Male:* red mustache. *Female:* no mustache.

STATUS: Very common summer resident in suitable habitat throughout the region; uncommon in winter.

Previously these two varieties, the Eastern Yellow-shafted Flicker and the Western Red-shafted Flicker, were considered to be separate species. However, because they interbreed in areas where their ranges overlap, the two varieties have been lumped together as a single species. The yellow-shafted variety is a bird of the east, with the western limit of its range reaching approximately to the east edge of the Black Hills. The red-shafted variety is a bird of the west and its range extends east to meet the range of the yellow-shafted. Where the two ranges meet, hybrids of the two varieties are not uncommon, so intermediate plumages are sometimes seen.

Northern Flickers reside virtually anywhere there are trees, but they prefer woodlots, orchards, open woodlands, urban environments, and burned areas in dense forests. Flickers eat berries but feed mostly on ants and other insects they find by probing the ground rather than chipping wood.

As with many migratory species, males arrive back on the nesting grounds before the females. The males begin their territorial drumming almost immediately and utilize a wide variety of structures, including snags, power poles, metal chimneys, roof vents, and even the sides of houses, much to the chagrin of the human inhabitants.

Both sexes return to their old territories each year and seek new nest sites. Once the pair-bond is formed, they excavate a new nesting cavity in suitable trees, utility poles, and sometimes even in the sides of buildings.

The male does most of the excavation. When he is finished, the female lays six to eight eggs and incubation begins. Both sexes incubate, with the male taking over the duties at night. The young hatch after about eleven days and are fed regurgitated insects, with the male making more visits to the nest than the female. The young begin meeting the adults at the nest hole after a couple weeks and fledge at twenty-six days. The young stay with the parents and continue to be fed by them for some time after leaving the nest.

Abandoned flicker holes are a vital source of nesting sites for other cavity nesters that are unable to excavate on their own, including small owl species, Buffleheads, American Kestrels, Eastern Bluebirds, and European Starlings.

Northern Flicker (red-shafted)

Northern Flicker (yellow-shafted)
—Photo by Tom J. Ulrich

Female Northern
Flicker with chick

PERCHING BIRDS
ORDER PASSERIFORMES

This order includes almost three-fifths of all living birds. Both size extremes, the 2-foot-long Common Raven and the 4- to 6-inch kinglets, live in this region. Some of the most adaptive and intelligent members of the bird world are passerines. The common feature among the perching birds is feet with four highly moveable toes, three toes pointing forward and one backward, that are ideally suited to gripping a twig, branch, wire, reed, or grass stem. Muscles and tendons automatically tighten their grip if the bird begins to fall backward.

Tyrant flycatcher: Western Wood-Pewee

Tyrant Flycatchers (Family Tyrannidae) include the flycatchers, pewees, phoebes, and kingbirds. The family is named "Tyrant" because they fiercely defend their nesting territories. They are named "flycatchers" for their habit of catching flying insects on the wing.

Shrikes (Family Laniidae) are songbirds that act like birds of prey. They feed on large insects, small lizards, mice, and small birds, which they kill with their powerful hook-tipped bill.

Jays and Crows (Family Corvidae) are large (10 to 25 inches) and conspicuous (black, blue, gray, green, or black-and-white), intelligent, and boisterous birds who adapt extremely well to changing conditions.

Gray Jay

Bank Swallow

Larks (Family Alaudidae) are inhabitants of the short-grass prairies and other areas with short, sparse grasses, where they walk while feeding on insects or seeds, and build their cup-shaped nests under a tuft of grass. Of particular note are flight songs.

Swallows (Family Hirundinidae) are small, fast-flying, streamlined birds that catch and eat insects in flight.

Black-capped Chickadee

Chickadees (Family Paridae) are tame, cheery, and gregarious little birds, and year-round residents who commonly visit bird feeders.

Nuthatches (Family Sittidae) are small birds with short tails, long wings, and long, slightly upturned bills. They glean the bark for insects, spiders, and larvae, and also eat the nuts and seeds of conifers.

House Wren with spider

Wrens (Family Troglodytidae) are small, brown, active birds with slender bills that feed almost exclusively on insects, which they glean from stems and leaves of shrubby vegetation.

Dippers (Family Cinclidae) orient their lives almost completely around the water, even foraging underwater for aquatic insects and insect larvae.

Thrushes (Family Turdidae) are small to medium-sized songbirds with flutelike songs that live on a mixed diet of insects, invertebrates, and plant materials.

Mockingbirds (Family Mimidae) are superb songsters and often sing from a conspicuous perch. Their neutral colors—grays and slate or plain brown—provide camouflage. The family names "Mimidae" and "Mockingbirds" come from the amazing ability these birds have to mimic the songs of other birds.

*Thrush:
Mountain Bluebird*

Starling with young

Starlings (Family Sturnidae) are an Old World family of birds with stout, straight bills and large, strong feet and legs—equipment ideally suited to birds that feed on virtually anything that can be located while walking on the ground. One species was brought to New York from Europe by a man who wanted to introduce to North America all the birds mentioned by Shakespeare.

Waxwings (Family Bombycillidae) are gregarious birds with prominent crests and soft silky plumage in muted colors; they were named "waxwings" because of the waxy tips on the wing coverts.

Warblers (Family Parulidae) are small, often brightly colored birds that pick insects from leaves and twigs of trees and shrubs with their slender, pointed bills.

Bohemian Waxwing

Tanagers (Family Thraupidae) are predominantly tropical birds—of 242 species, only a couple wander into the temperate habitats of the world. They sport stout bills, and the males have brilliantly colored plumage.

Warbler: Common Yellowthroat

Sparrows (Family Emberizidae) are small (four to seven inches) birds with predominantly dull gray or brown plumage. You can identify these birds primarily on the basis of subtle but distinctive plumage characteristics, including face, crown, and breast patterns. One or more species of sparrow can be found in virtually all types of habitats in the region.

Male Western Tanager

Buntings and Grosbeaks (Family Cardinalidae) are small, seed-eating birds with conical bills that are pointed

White-crowned Sparrow

at the tip for picking up seeds and heavy at the base for cracking them.

Blackbirds and Orioles (Family Icteridae) are highly visible and vocal birds with strong, sharply pointed bills that enable them to eat a wide variety of food including insects, seeds, grain, and berries.

Male Lazuli Bunting

*Female House Finch
with cherries*

Finches (Family Fringillidae) are seedeaters with stout bills. They use their tongues to peel and discard the husks to get to the seeds. While most other birds rely heavily on insects to provide enough protein to their rapidly growing youngsters, some of the finches (crossbills, siskins and redpolls) raise their young exclusively on a diet of seeds.

Weaver Finches (Family Passeridae) are primarily an Old World family of birds named for some of its members, who weave the largest and most complex nests in the bird world. Two introduced species represent this family in North America.

TYRANT FLYCATCHERS

Willow Flycatcher

Empidonax traillii

FIELD MARKS: 6 inches. Brownish green back, whitish underparts; faint eye ring; orange lower mandible.

STATUS: Ranges across the northern U.S. from coast to coast; uncommon to locally common summer resident throughout most of this region; rare in eastern WY, western NE, the BH, and BLNP.

The Willow Flycatcher occupies a wide variety of "edge" habitats—from brushy fields and weed lots to willow thickets and open woodlands. The territory is usually near water where the males may be seen singing from high perches. Like the rest of their family, Willow Flycatchers also use conspicuous perches as a base for spotting flying insects and then fluttering out to snatch them out of the air.

Willow Flycatchers nest in late June and early July. The female places her small, well-hidden, compact nest low in a tree or bush, usually within 4 to 6 feet of the ground. She incubates the clutch of three or four eggs.

Although you will easily recognize the Willow Flycatcher as a member of the *Empidonax* genus of flycatchers, you will most likely run into difficulty separating it from the other species of the same genus. Experts generally agree that *Empidonax* flycatchers often display greater differences in plumage between individuals within a species than they do between species. All the *Empidonax* flycatchers look much like the bird in the photograph, with wing bars, eye ring, and greenish plumage. Their songs best distinguish them in the field. Identify the Willow Flycatcher by its dry "*FITZ-bew*" call, which emphasizes the first syllable. The "*fee-BEE-o*" call of the very similar Alder Flycatcher stresses the second syllable.

——SIMILAR SPECIES——

Western Wood-Pewee

Contopus sordidulus

FIELD MARKS: 8 inches. Dusky gray brown plumage; **two white wing bars; no eye ring; dull, dark bill.** *Call:* a nasal descending *"pheer."*

STATUS: Ranges from the West Coast to the western third of ND, SD, and NE; uncommon to common summer resident throughout the region; common summer resident in the BH; rare in BLNP.

The Western Wood-Pewee often perches on a dead branch at the edge of a forest clearing. It periodically flits out to snatch a bee, wasp, ant, fly, or other insect from the air with an audible snap of its bill. In the Black Hills, it inhabits open pine forests.

This bird beautifully crafts its nest, camouflaging it with lichens, in a crotch of a horizontal branch between 15 and 75 feet above the ground. Perhaps because the nests are placed in the open and not hidden by surrounding vegetation, Brown-headed Cowbirds often lay eggs in wood-pewee nests (see pp. 198–99).

Willow Flycatcher in nest

Western Wood-Pewee

Eastern Kingbird
Tyrannus tyrannus

FIELD MARKS: 9 inches. Slate gray head and upperparts; concealed red crown patch; **white underparts**; broad, fan-shaped tail **tipped with broad white band.**

STATUS: Ranges from the East Coast almost to the West Coast; common summer resident throughout the region; less common in the west and in the BH; not recorded in BLNP.

As it flies with short, quick wing beats, the Eastern Kingbird's wings seem to quiver. Conspicuous, noisy, and aggressive, a kingbird will fearlessly attack a hawk, crow, or any other bird that enters its territory. This bird frequents open country with scattered trees and perches with good views for spotting insects, often near water. It waits on an exposed perch, occasionally darting into the air to snap up an insect, often with an audible click of its bill. In addition to the more than 200 species of insects it eats, the Eastern Kingbird dines on the fruits and seeds of more than 40 different plant species.

Males arrive on the nesting grounds in early May, about the time insects become plentiful. They often return to the same territory as the previous year and soon begin their aerial displays and harsh screams to repel other males and attract females. After pair-bonds are formed, fights between pairs on adjacent territories are common.

The site chosen for the nest is often in a lone tree less than 20 feet above the ground. The male helps build the bulky nest, but the female does the incubating. Both sexes help feed the young, although the female seems to be the more active parent. After about two weeks, the young are mature enough to leave the nest. For the next week, they can often be seen moving about together and perching as a group, waiting for their parents to feed them. Within another week, they are catching insects on their own.

——SIMILAR SPECIES——

Western Kingbird
Tyrannus verticalis

FIELD MARKS: 9 inches. Pale gray head and upperparts; concealed red crown patch; white throat; **pale yellow underparts**; white edges on tail.

STATUS: Ranges from West Coast to the eastern limits of this region; common summer resident throughout the region, including BLNP; less common in the BH.

The Western Kingbird nests slightly later and is less aggressive than its eastern cousin. It frequents dry, open country with scattered trees and shrubs, and at times even shares its nesting tree with others of its kind. It seems to have a propensity to place nest sites on or near electric transformers and substations.

Eastern Kingbird

Western Kingbird

SHRIKES

Loggerhead Shrike   *Lanius ludovicianus*

FIELD MARKS: 9 inches. Gray, white, and black plumage; **heavy, all-black hooked bill**; big head; broad black mask **that meets over the bill**; rapid wing beats; long, thin tail.

STATUS: Ranges all across the U.S.; fairly common summer resident throughout the region, including BLNP; less common in the east and in the BH.

Loggerhead Shrikes feed on large insects, small lizards, mice, and small birds, which they hunt from a perch. Once a shrike captures its prey, it dispatches it with its large hooked bill and then usually eats it immediately or feeds it to its nestlings. Lacking the powerful feet and talons of the true raptors, shrikes impale their prey on thorns or barbed wire to secure it while they tear off bite-sized pieces. Shrikes will often leave the impaled prey item and return to eat it later.

The Loggerhead Shrike inhabits open country, where you can see it sitting quietly on a telephone wire beside a road or perching on the highest twig of a tree or bush. Scattered or clustered trees or shrubs—shelterbelts, farmsteads, and hedgerows—provide the perches and mix of trees and open country that they prefer.

Nesting may occur in this region from late April through the end of June. Territories are rather large, with an average of at least 400 yards between adjacent nests. Both sexes participate in building the bulky nest deep in a low bush, providing a secure home for the four to seven youngsters. It is usually located less than 10 feet above the ground and well hidden in dense foliage, often in a thorny tree. The female assumes responsibility for the incubation and the male feeds her on the nest. Incubation takes about sixteen days, and it is another seventeen days before the youngsters fledge.

As winter approaches, birds in this region drift to the south and are often replaced by Loggerhead or Northern Shrikes that nested farther north.

Loggerhead Shrike

JAYS AND CROWS

Gray Jay
Perisoreus canadensis

FIELD MARKS: 12 inches. ***Adult:* gray plumage; short bill;** white forehead; black nape; long tail. ***Juvenile:*** sooty black.

STATUS: Ranges across the taiga of northern Canada, down the Rocky Mountains. Fairly common resident of the higher elevation forests of the BH; not recorded in BLNP.

HOT SPOTS: Black Hills, SD.

Also called Canada Jays, these residents of dense pine and spruce forests are unafraid of humans. Omnivorous, they eat a wide variety of natural foods—lichens, grasshoppers, berries, mice, eggs, and young of other birds. People picnicking or camping in woods where these birds are found soon learn that Gray Jays have no second thoughts about brazenly stealing bread, crackers, peanuts, and other tidbits from picnic tables—they have even been known to steal bacon from the frying pan. Their nickname, "camp robbers," is well deserved!

Gray Jays regularly cache food. They produce a special saliva that binds food together so the mass can be firmly held in position among conifer foliage. Later, when pickings are slimmer, the jays return to their caches to feed.

Gray Jays have loose, fluffy plumage that allows almost silent flight. There is something almost mystical about having one or more of these birds silently materialize nearby during a quiet winter outing.

Gray Jays nest very early in the year, when the snow is still on the ground and the temperatures are low. They hide their bulky nests in pine or spruce trees—often less than 10 feet above the ground. Both sexes help build the nest, and the female incubates the three or four eggs on her own. The male provides most of the food for the first few days of the chicks' lives. The young fledge in about fifteen days, and the family group often lives and forages together until the next breeding cycle begins.

Not loud and raucous like the call of some jays, the Gray Jay's call is generally a soft "*weeoo*" or "*weef weef weef weef.*"

——SIMILAR SPECIES——

Clark's Nutcracker
Nucifraga columbiana

FIELD MARKS: 13 inches. Gray plumage; **long, sharply pointed bill; black-and-white wings;** short tail. **Flashy white wing and tail patches visible in flight.**

STATUS: Ranges throughout the Rocky Mountain West. Uncommon winter visitor in the BH; may occasionally stay and breed; not recorded in BLNP.

HOT SPOTS: Black Hills, SD.

Look for Clark's Nutcrackers in openings near extensive stands of conifers, often near the timberline, where they use their long bills to extract the seeds from treetop cones. They also gather grubs from the bark, insects from the air, and scraps and handouts from picnickers. Nutcrackers cache food like some of the other jays, returning later to retrieve the stored tidbits, even from under 2 feet of snow. These caches of partially digested seeds are one of the primary sources of seedling regeneration for nut-producing pines (whitebark and limber pine).

Gray Jay

Clark's Nutcracker

Blue Jay   *Cyanocitta cristata*

FIELD MARKS: 10 inches. Conspicuous crest; **white head with blue cap;** pale blue back; white breast; **blue wings with white patches; blue tail with white patches.**

STATUS: Ranges from the East Coast to western part of this region; continues to pioneer new areas and extend its range further west; fairly common resident in region; less common to the west; absent from the upper BH; rare in BLNP.

The Blue Jay is among the best known of the eastern birds. Large and conspicuous, this raucous and intelligent bird thrives in spite of drastic changes in its environment and persecution by humans. The stout, pointed bill is the perfect tool for its opportunistic feeding habits.

Widely distributed in deciduous forests, cities, towns, suburban areas, and parks, the Blue Jay seems to prefer grassland areas with scattered clumps of trees. For most of the year, it is noisy and boisterous—uttering its "*jay, jay*" call with no apparent fear of being noticed. In the spring, however, just before nesting, Blue Jays become very secretive. As part of their courtship, the male brings branches to the female, which she begins to fashion into a nest. She may start several false nests in different locations before she begins work on the actual nest. The male may help gather sticks, which he usually breaks off of trees.

The nest itself is a large, bulky structure, well hidden in the crotch or outer branches of a tree—often a conifer. The main structure is built of twigs, interspersed with bark and leaves and lined with small roots. While the nest is vigorously defended against predators—cats, squirrels, owls, and hawks—it is not defended against other Blue Jays. In May the female lays her eggs and incubates them, while the male feeds her on the nest. The young fledge in about five weeks, and the adults continue to feed them for another two months.

The breeding pair stays on the nesting area throughout the winter, but eventually the young disperse in groups. Jays are perfectly willing to visit feeders to supplement their diet, and seem to prefer sunflower seeds and cracked corn scattered on the ground.

——SIMILAR SPECIES——

Pinyon Jay   *Gymnorhinus cyanocephalus*

FIELD MARKS: 9 inches. No crest; **uniform steel blue color.**

STATUS: Ranges through the western mountain ranges; common in the lower elevations of the BH and similar habitats in western NE.

HOT SPOTS: Black Hills, SD; Fort Robinson SP, Crawford, NE; Chadron SP, Chadron, NE.

The only other blue jay in this region, Pinyon Jays are highly gregarious, noisy, and boisterous. Often gathering in flocks of fifty or more, they wander through the drier, scattered pine forests of the Black Hills. The call is a raucous "*queh queh queh.*"

Blue Jay —Photo by Alan G. Nelson

Pinyon Jay

Black-billed Magpie

Pica hudsonia

FIELD MARKS: 20 inches. Large; looks **black and white** from a distance and in poor light; shines greenish blue metallic when close-up; **long tail.**

STATUS: Ranges from the West Coast to eastern third of this region. Fairly common resident in western two-thirds of this region, including the BH; abundant in BLNP.

This inhabitant of open country is common and highly visible in grassland-badland habitats of the region. Black-billed Magpies often travel in small family groups of six to ten birds. They prefer open country with a scattering of trees. There, they forage in sagebrush, croplands, and pasturelands.

Bold, inquisitive, but always suspicious, magpies live in the presence of humans but never really seem to accept them. Magpies may feed regularly at the suet feeder or the dog's dish, but never if people are nearby. If magpies live near you, it will not take you long to learn to recognize their loud *"mahg"* call.

Magpies are ground feeders. They walk with a distinctively graceful yet jerky movement, usually holding their tail up at a slight angle. When they need to move faster, they hop. Omnivorous like the other jays, they eat a wide variety of food, from carrion to grasshoppers and other insects, insect larvae and pupae, snakes, mice, fruit, and grains. They can regularly be seen on the backs of large mammals—both wild and domestic—where they pick and eat the parasites they find. One of their less desirable habits is eating the eggs and young of other birds.

About mid-March or April, pairs form and begin nest building, which appears to be part of the courtship as the male brings nesting material to the female and she places it in the crotch of a thorny shrub or conifer. This process goes on more than a month. When complete, the large, dome-shaped mass of sticks with a side entrance may be 2 or more feet high. Inside, a mud cup lined with rootlets, grass, and hair provides a cradle for the four to seven eggs.

The female does all the incubation for the sixteen days until hatching, but the male regularly brings her food at the nest. Both sexes help feed, and the young fledge in about four weeks. After fledging, the short-tailed youngsters are easily recognized as juveniles and are soon foraging for themselves. The family group usually stays together and they begin to wander away from the nesting area.

The following year, a new nest is usually constructed and the old nest left for other inhabitants. American Kestrels, Sharp-shinned Hawks, owls, ducks, Mourning Doves, House Sparrows, and grackles are all known to use old magpie nests. Mice also often make use of the old nests to raise their young.

Black-billed Magpie

American Crow

Corvus brachyrhynchos

FIELD MARKS: 20 inches. **Jet black plumage; stout bill; call is** the familiar *"caw, caw, caw."*

STATUS: Common resident throughout the region, including the BH; uncommon in BLNP.

American Crows usually inhabit farming country with a mix of cultivated fields, pastures, scattered woodlots, and fence rows. Although wary of humans, crows are beginning to take up residence in many cities and towns. With their nests wedged in the forks of trees 20 to 60 feet overhead, the birds are secure from human harassment but still have access to the food sources provided by humans—particularly around parks and restaurant dumpsters. Outside of town, crows feed on displaced grasshoppers and mice in newly mown hayfields, waste grain in harvested grain fields, and choice tidbits in area landfills.

Usually loud throughout the winter and while courting, crows become very quiet during the nesting period. Sometime between April and June, a small group of crows—the breeding pair and their young from the previous year (crows do not breed until their second year)—begins to hang around a small area that will be the site of the nest.

The male of the pair breaks branches directly off trees and brings them to the female. She begins to construct the nest, although she may begin several preliminary nests before completing one. With both birds working, a large, sturdy platform of branches and twigs is built to hold the large egg cup, which is lined with rootlets, hair, and feathers. The average of five young hatch in eighteen days and fledge thirty-six days after that.

After the nesting season, family groups begin to gather in loose flocks and wander through the countryside in search of food. As winter approaches, more and more groups of crows begin roosting at a few large communal roosting sites. The roost may contain from a few hundred to a few hundred thousand birds! They use these favored roosts for weeks at a time and may reuse them from year to year—sometimes becoming a serious nuisance to people living in close proximity.

Each morning, the crows disperse in small groups to forage across the countryside. Some groups may go as far as 50 miles each day to feed. By midafternoon, they begin their return flights back to roost. By late afternoon, these loose flocks have congregated at a number of preroost sites to feed and socialize. At dusk, they make their final flight to the roost along established flight lines, with long lines of crows passing a particular location a few at a time for an hour or more.

American Crow

Larks

Horned Lark
Eremophila alpestris

FIELD MARKS: 8 inches. Brown above, white below; **black crown, facial stripe, and breast band;** slender bill; horns not always visible; yellowish wash on face and throat.

STATUS: Ranges through suitable habitat all across Mexico, the U.S., and Canada; abundant to common summer resident in short-grass–sagebrush areas throughout region; variable winter resident (sometimes seen in flocks of thousands); abundant in BLNP.

Members of the lark family inhabit areas with low-growing, sparse grasses. On the ground larks walk rather than hop as most birds do. Horned Larks rarely perch above ground, although they may occasionally pause on a fence wire or low shrub for a few seconds before dropping back to the ground. When feeding, they walk or run back and forth over the ground in search of weed seeds, waste grain, and insects.

In this region, Horned Larks establish territories early, often in January and February. The males sometimes advertise their presence by singing their weak songs while circling as high as 800 feet above the ground. At other times, they may sing from a perch on the ground. The songs seem to be more for courtship than for territorial defense. However, the males do actively defend their rather large territories—sometimes over 4 acres—against other males.

Once paired, the female locates her nest under a tuft of grass—the only cover available in the wide expanses of open, barren country the Horned Lark calls home. Using her bill and feet, the female digs or enlarges a slight hollow and lines it with fine grasses to hold her three to four finely speckled, off-white eggs.

Nests with eggs have been found in South Dakota as early as April 9 and as late as July, but most eggs are probably laid in May. About ten days after hatching, the young have half-grown flight feathers and leave the nest when they are only able to fly short distances. By the time fall rolls around, they have joined with juveniles and adults from nearby to form large flocks. These flocks may be joined by other flocks—sometimes of other species such as longspurs and Snow Buntings. In winter, these large mixed flocks can often be seen in cultivated fields and along roadsides as they wander in search of food.

Horned Lark

Swallows

Purple Martin
Progne subis

FIELD MARKS: 8 inches. ***Male:*** **purplish black plumage.** ***Female:*** **dull purplish black above,** grayish below. ***In flight:*** long, triangular wings; long, shallowly forked tail.

STATUS: Ranges from East Coast to eastern half of this region; also found close to West Coast; common summer resident in eastern half of this region; occasional migrant in the BH; not reported in BLNP.

This tame and beloved member of the swallow family is well known for its willingness to use birdhouses. Native Americans attracted these birds to their villages by hanging gourds for them to nest in. Purple Martins traditionally used old woodpecker holes and small pockets in cliffs. As those sites became scarce, they readily adapted to man-made cavities. Colonial nesters, most Purple Martins now use multicompartment martin houses. The most successful martin houses are located in open settings, between 15 and 20 above the ground, with nearby wires or bare branches for perching.

A sure sign of spring for many people, Purple Martins arrive up to two months before beginning to nest. The males choose a nesting compartment and guard it by sitting in the opening. When the females arrive, they choose a male that occupies a compartment.

Sometime in May both sexes begin collecting plant materials to build the nest. The female usually lays four to five eggs and assumes all incubation duties. When she leaves to feed, the male guards the nest by sitting in the opening. The eggs hatch in about fifteen days.

Both sexes help feed the young. Purple Martins capture most of their insect food in flight, but also pick up ants, wasps, beetles, and other crawling insects from the ground. Long, pointed wings provide them with the maneuverability needed to scoop erratically flying insects out of the air. Facial bristles help guide prey into their large mouths.

Purple Martins also drink on the wing, skimming their lower jaw through the surface of nearby lakes or streams and scooping up water. They bathe by wetting their plumage as they fly over.

Purple martins leave the area again in late August. The young have a strong tendency to return to the site where they were raised. This results in added stability for established nesting locations, but tends to limit the colonization of new sites. Bird lovers wishing to attract Purple Martins may need to exercise some patience until the birds find the martin house and establish a new colony.

Male Purple Martin —Photo by Tom J. Ulrich

Violet-green Swallow   *Tachycineta thalassina*

FIELD MARKS: 5 inches. **Dark upperparts with a green and purplish sheen,** white below; white patches on side of rump almost meet over the tail; **white on sides of neck extends up on neck and over eyes.**

STATUS: Ranges from the West Coast through the western half of this region; common summer resident in the BH and similar habitats in western NE and eastern WY; rare in BLNP.

Found only in the west, Violet-green Swallows frequent forests and steep-walled canyons. Unusually early migrants, they may be on their nesting grounds for a month before actually beginning to nest.

After pairing sometime in June, the female chooses a tree cavity or suitable crevice in a cliff. Violet-green Swallows have begun to invade man-made habitats and nest in crevices in buildings not already occupied by House Sparrows. The female provides the bulk of the nesting material. She begins laying an egg a day until her clutch of four to seven eggs is complete. Two weeks later, the eggs hatch and the female broods her young and provides most of their food for the first ten days. The young fledge in a little over three weeks and do not return to the nest once they leave.

Violet-green Swallows fly south in late August to winter along the Pacific Coast of Mexico.

---SIMILAR SPECIES---

Tree Swallow   *Tachycineta bicolor*

FIELD MARKS: 6 inches. *Male:* **steely blue black** above; white below; **white on neck does not extend above eye, which is entirely within the dark crown feathers;** triangular wings; squarish tail. *Female:* similar, but with slightly duller colors.

STATUS: Ranges all across the northern two-thirds of the U.S. and Canada; uncommon to local summer resident at lower elevations in the region; local in the BH; rare in BLNP.

Tree Swallows are the first swallows to arrive in spring and the last to head south in fall. They prefer more open country, often near water, than do their smaller cousins, the Violet-green Swallows. Cavity nesters like the Violet-greens, Tree Swallows often nest in aspens and compete with Mountain Bluebirds, Northern Flickers, and House Wrens for available cavities. They readily accept bluebird houses and now compete with bluebirds for those nesting spaces. Birdhouses occupied by swallows are easily recognized by the presence of feathers in the nest. They defend their nesting space by repeatedly dive-bombing trespassers.

The only swallows to winter regularly in the United States, Tree Swallows from this region spend the cold season in Florida or elsewhere along the Gulf of Mexico.

Violet-green Swallow

Male Tree Swallow

Barn Swallow

Hirundo rustica

FIELD MARKS: 7 inches. *Male:* metallic blue-black above; red-brown forehead and breast; deeply forked tail. *Female:* similar but with slightly duller colors.

STATUS: Ranges all across North America; abundant summer resident wherever suitable nesting structures are available, including the BH and BLNP.

On long, pointed wings, Barn Swallows swoop and glide, often skimming the surface of the water, occasionally dipping to pick up a bug or take a sip of water. Short legs and tiny feet enable them to perch on wires and thin branches but are almost never used to walk.

Relatively tolerant of humans, Barn Swallows, as their name suggests, readily nest in buildings or birdhouses. Formerly limited by a shortage of suitable cliffs for nesting, these birds have ranged more widely with the proliferations of barns and other buildings. This willingness to live near humans has made the graceful Barn Swallow one of the most familiar and best-loved birds in North America.

Shortly after arriving back in this region in the spring, usually in May or June, both sexes begin making appearances at puddles or on muddy shorelines to collect mud to construct their cup-shaped nests. The pellet of mud is carried back to a sheltered eave or inside a barn or open shed and plastered to the side of a wall, joist, or rafter near the roof or ceiling. The mud nest sticks together very well, but may have strands of horsehair and other material added to help hold it together. The mud cup is usually built within a week and lined with feathers before the four or five eggs are laid.

The female incubates while the male spends his time perching on nearby utility lines or feeding overhead on flying insects. He diligently defends the nest area from intruders—not an ingratiating trait when the nest is near a building entranceway! The young hatch in two weeks and leave the nest three weeks later. The pair may raise two broods in a single season, sometimes making a double-decker nest by adding more mud and relining it with feathers.

As fall approaches, Barn Swallows gather in large flocks to feed, roost, and migrate. By September, they have left the region for warmer climes in the south.

——SIMILAR SPECIES——

Cliff Swallow

Petrochelidon pyrrhonota

FIELD MARKS: 6 inches. Black crown, back, wings, and tail; **dark rufous throat, neck, and rump;** pale forehead; **dark, square-tipped tail.**

STATUS: Ranges all across North America; abundant summer resident in this region wherever suitable nesting structures are available, including the BH and BLNP.

Cliff Swallows build their mud nests on the outsides of bridges, barns, hotels, observation towers, and other buildings, as well as on cliffs. The gourd-shaped nests are sometimes stacked on top of one another, and colonies may contain hundreds of pairs. Cliff Swallows can be seen in this region from April to September.

Barn Swallow

Pair of Cliff Swallows

CHICKADEES

Black-capped Chickadee   *Poecile atricapillus*

FIELD MARKS: 5 inches. Small; gray and white plumage; **black cap and bib;** white cheeks; buffy flanks; ***"chick-a-dee-dee-dee"* call is diagnostic.**

STATUS: Ranges all across the northern U.S.; common resident throughout the region, including the BH and BLNP.

Spritely little birds, Black-capped Chickadees prefer deciduous forests, river courses, and woodlots. Very tolerant of humans, in winter they are among the most common visitors to bird feeders, easily attracted by suet and sunflower seeds. Their hesitant, undulating flight is a common sight as they make trip after trip to and from the feeders. After picking a sunflower seed from the feeder, they fly to a nearby tree or bush, wedge the seed in a handy crack or crevice, and chip it open with their bill. They also search the twigs and bark of trees and bushes for dormant insects and spider eggs. Black-capped Chickadees are year-round residents and live in flocks (often with other species such as nuthatches) in the winter. As spring approaches, they often pair with their mates from the previous year. Courtship involves the *"Fee-bee"* song sung by the male.

Black-capped Chickadees are cavity nesters but are unable to excavate a hollow themselves unless the wood is well rotted. They may remodel an abandoned woodpecker hole. The female begins the excavation but the male helps prepare the cavity. When the female is satisfied, they line the cavity with hair, feathers, or other soft materials. Chickadees accept birdhouses, though less readily than wrens and bluebirds. Partially filling the box with wood chips or sawdust, which the birds can then rearrange or "excavate" to their liking, seems to make the house more attractive.

The female lays an egg a day until the clutch of four to six eggs is complete. She incubates and the male feeds her at the nest. Twelve days after the last egg was laid, the young hatch. The youngsters grow rapidly on a rich diet of insects, and fledge in about sixteen days. The young continue to beg from the parents after leaving the nest but soon are well able to forage for themselves. They remain with the parents for about another month.

——SIMILAR SPECIES——

Mountain Chickadee   *Poecile gambeli*

FIELD MARKS: 6 inches. Small; gray and white plumage; black cap and bib; **white eyebrows;** white cheeks. Call is a hoarse *"chick-a-dee."*

STATUS: Ranges across western North America; casual visitor in the BH and western edge of this region.

Although it is often seen with Black-capped Chickadees and shares many of the same habitats, Mountain Chickadees seem to prefer drier, more open coniferous woods at slightly higher elevations. Mountain Chickadees build their nests in rotting stumps or snags and raise two and sometimes three broods, with as many as nine youngsters in each brood.

Black-capped Chickadee

Mountain Chickadee

NUTHATCHES

White-breasted Nuthatch *Sitta carolinensis*

FIELD MARKS: 6 inches. Black crown; **white face and underparts**; blue-gray back.

STATUS: Ranges across most of the U.S.; fairly common resident in deciduous habitats throughout the region and in the BH; uncommon in BLNP.

Nuthatches live their lives on tree trunks and larger branches, gleaning insects, spiders, and larvae from the bark. An enlarged hind toe enables them to hunt head-down. They use only their feet and legs and do not use their tails as a brace like the Brown Creeper and the woodpeckers do. The largest of the nuthatches, the White-breasted Nuthatch occupies a wide variety of habitats across the region. Besides insects they eat nuts and seeds of conifers. They are easily attracted to bird feeders by suet and sunflower seeds.

Nuthatches are monogamous and maintain their pair-bonds throughout the year, and they also defend their territories year-round. The loud "*yank-yank*" call is easy to recognize and is heard more often as nesting season approaches. The female chooses the nest site and does all the nest building. White-breasted Nuthatches rarely use birdhouses, preferring to prepare their own nesting cavity. Knotholes between 15 and 50 feet above the ground are often used as an entrance hole. The finishing touch involves "bill-sweeping" at the entrance hole. Both sexes rub their bills at the entrance while holding an insect.

——SIMILAR SPECIES——

Red-breasted Nuthatch *Sitta canadensis*

FIELD MARKS: 4 inches. Small; blue-gray back; black crown; black eye line; white eyebrow; **rufous underparts.** *Female:* duller.

STATUS: Ranges throughout the U.S.; common migrant throughout the region; common resident in the BH and BLNP.

These birds inhabit open stands of lodgepole and Douglas-fir at higher elevations. Red-breasted Nuthatches excavate nesting cavities in conifers or conifer snags and, for reasons unknown to humans, smear the entrance hole with pitch. The birds typically fly directly into the hole without perching or pausing at the entrance.

Pygmy Nuthatch *Sitta pygmaea*

FIELD MARKS: 4 inches. Brownish head; **black eye line**; bluish gray back; cream-colored undersides.

STATUS: Ranges in selected habitats in the west; uncommon resident in the BH only.

The smallest of the nuthatches, the Pygmy Nuthatch searches clusters of pine needles at the ends of branches for insects and pine seeds. The quiet habits and soft twittering voice of this seemingly unafraid bird make it an inconspicuous resident of yellow pine habitats. It can nest in cavities too small for other species to use. It travels in flocks much more than the other nuthatches.

White-breasted Nuthatch —Photo by Tom J. Ulrich
Inset: *Red-breasted Nuthatch*

Pygmy Nuthatch —Photo by Tom J. Ulrich

WRENS

House Wren
Troglodytes aedon

FIELD MARKS: 5 inches. Gray brown above, pale brown below; slender bill; barred tail; beautiful, bubbling song.

STATUS: Ranges across northern U.S. and Canada; common to abundant summer resident throughout the region except the upper BH; common in BLNP.

House Wrens are small, brown, active birds with a habit of cocking their tails over their backs. Found near thickets in open tree stands, near forest edges, in old orchards, near old trees, and in run-down buildings, they prefer to remain hidden, but become fearless when intruders venture too close to their nest.

In the spring male House Wrens establish territories by singing their melodious songs from prominent perches, altering their song depending on the sex of the intruder. When a singing male recognizes an intruding wren as a female, his voice becomes high and squeaky. As an added attraction, he vibrates his wings as he sings.

When the male is not singing, he often occupies himself by filling a half dozen or more potential nest cavities with 4-inch sticks. Wrens compete aggressively with other cavity-nesting species. They may even evict nesting birds by puncturing their eggs and throwing out all their nest material.

The female explores the potential nest sites with the male and eventually chooses one. Occasionally, females select some rather strange places to nest—an old tin can, a cow skull, a pump spigot, a pocket of a discarded coat, and a mailbox have all been used to raise young. Once she has chosen the cavity, the female removes the male's sticks and replaces them with twigs she gathers herself.

The male rarely enters the nest, although he does bring food to the female while she is incubating the five or six eggs. The male may perform the wing quiver while he feeds the female. His song becomes quieter and shorter while the young are in the nest.

——SIMILAR SPECIES——

Marsh Wren
Cistothorus palustris

FIELD MARKS: 5 inches. Brown plumage; solid rufous crown; white "eyebrows"; long, decurved bill; white-streaked breast.

STATUS: Abundant summer resident in eastern part of region; local in other areas of suitable habitat; rare in the BH.

Marsh Wrens are conspicuous residents of cattail and bulrush marshes and wet roadside ditches. After building numerous (up to thirty-five in some cases) domed nests to attract a female, the male perches high on a rush or cattail and launches his sputtering calls and trills, often with his tail cocked beyond the vertical over his back. When won over, the female moves into one of the nests and the rest remain vacant. Most Marsh Wrens fly to Mexico or the southern border states to spend the winter.

House Wren

Marsh Wren

DIPPERS
American Dipper
Cinclus mexicanus

FIELD MARKS: 8 inches. Small and **plump; slate gray;** short, stubby tail; **bobs up and down.**

STATUS: Listed as threatened in the BH in 1996. Ranges along suitable mountain streams throughout the west; locally common permanent resident along the rushing, tumbling, icy cold mountain streams of the BH.

HOT SPOTS: Roughlock Falls and Spearfish Creek, BH.

You are very unlikely to see an American Dipper unless you are looking in or around a rocky, swift mountain stream. There you may see them wading in shallow riffles with their heads submerged or bobbing up and down on a midstream rock, preparing to venture once more into the icy water in pursuit of aquatic insects. Even on extremely cold winter days, dippers wade in the shallows, sometimes disappearing under the ice in search of aquatic insects and tiny fish. When traveling upstream or downstream to foraging areas, the dipper flies over the water, seldom taking shortcuts over land.

The lives of dippers are almost totally oriented to water. Extremely soft, thick plumage and an exceptionally large preen gland, which produces oil to waterproof their feathers, allow them to endure cold temperatures and icy water with impunity. Movable flaps that cover their nostrils, nictitating membranes (transparent inner eyelids to protect their eyes), and strong feet and legs to grasp the rocky bottom enable the dipper to forage underwater for aquatic insects and larvae. They may also use their wings to hold themselves on the bottom, a habit that has led some observers to report that these birds "fly" underwater.

Courtship, in the form of wing quivering, chasing, and singing, peaks in April. Surprisingly, the dipper's pleasantly melodious song can often be heard over the roar of the water. When this flurry of activity settles down, the breeding pairs are well separated along the rivers and the female begins nest construction.

A bulky ball (8 to 12 inches in diameter) of woven moss with a side entrance, the nest is frequently placed where a constant spray keeps the moss damp and alive, forming a living, growing nest. Under an overhanging rock ledge, bridge, or even behind a waterfall are common locations.

Both sexes help build the nest or refurbish an old nest from a prior year, and the female incubates the three to six eggs. The male contributes by bringing food to the female while she is on the nest. The female continues to brood the altricial youngsters for about a week after hatching. As the young mature, they venture to the nest opening and eagerly poke their heads out to be fed. Dippers mature relatively slowly for their size and do not fledge until they are about twenty-five days old.

As the weather cools off, dippers begin to move to their winter waters. By November, they have set up their winter territories, which they will defend through February. These sometimes overlap the nesting territory, but often are on downstream, ice-free sections of the river.

American Dipper —Photo by Tom J. Ulrich

THRUSHES

Mountain Bluebird
Sialia currucoides

FIELD MARKS: 6 1/2 inches. *Male:* sky blue plumage, lightest on the breast and belly. *Female:* duller gray with blue tinge on wings.

STATUS: Ranges across the western U.S.; common summer breeder throughout MT, WY, and CO, in the western third of the Dakotas, and the western edge of NE; very common in the BH and BLNP.

HOT SPOTS: Teddy Roosevelt NP, ND; Black Hills, SD; Fort Robinson SP and Ponderosa WMA, NE.

The striking, azure blue Mountain Bluebird may arrive in this region in late March, often when snow is still on the ground. It selects a territory in open country—burned or cutover areas, open woodlands, or aspen clumps—near snags or other suitable nesting cavities. It defends its territory by singing from a prominent perch. In the absence of natural nesting cavities, Mountain Bluebirds readily accept nest boxes, whose widespread availability in recent years has increased populations dramatically.

The female builds the nest and both parents feed the young. Nest sites are usually no closer than about 300 feet to adjacent pairs. When other bluebirds enter the territory, the female defends the nest site while the male defends the periphery of the territory. Bluebirds lay between four and eight eggs, which hatch in just under two weeks. The young fledge about three weeks after hatching. In normal years most bluebird pairs raise two broods. In a few instances, the young of the first brood have been known to help feed the young of the second brood.

Mountain Bluebirds snap up insects, their main food, from the ground or out of the air. Unlike other bluebirds, Mountain Bluebirds often hover when pursuing insects. After raising the young the family groups form large flocks before heading south. A few may remain in the region through the winter.

——SIMILAR SPECIES——

Eastern Bluebird
Sialia sialis

FIELD MARKS: 6 inches. White belly. *Male:* deep blue back and wings; **orange throat** and breast; hunched appearance. *Female:* grayish; rust tint to breast; bluish wings and tail.

STATUS: Ranges across eastern North America; uncommon summer resident across the eastern two-thirds of ND, SD, and NE; rare in the BH, MT, and WY; uncommon in BLNP.

HOT SPOTS: J. Clark Salyer NWR, ND; Sand Lake NWR, BH, SD; Crescent Lake, NE.

The Eastern Bluebird is the only bluebird found east of this region. Growing numbers of birdhouses put out by concerned bird lovers have helped increase

Male Mountain Bluebird

Female Mountain Bluebird

populations, and this brightly colored bird is once more fairly common in much of its range.

Western Bluebird   *Sialia mexicana*

FIELD MARKS: 6 inches. ***Male:*** **deep blue throat,** back, and wings; rusty breast; **chestnut patch on upper back; blue belly;** hunched appearance. ***Female:*** grayish; rust tint to breast; bluish wings and tail; grayish belly.

STATUS: Ranges across the western U.S.; rare local breeder in this region and in the BH; absent from BLNP.

HOT SPOTS: Wildcat Hills SRA, Chadron SP, Chadron, NE.

Inhabitants of the middle to low elevations, Western Bluebirds frequent forest edges, open forest, roadsides, and farmlands. Not as migratory as Mountain Bluebirds, Western Bluebirds may winter on their breeding range or in nearby lowlands.

Male Eastern Bluebird

Male Western Bluebird

American Robin
Turdus migratorius

FIELD MARKS: 10 inches. Plump profile, black head; yellow bill; dark gray brown back; **dark red orange breast.**

STATUS: Common to abundant resident throughout the region.

Robins frequent virtually all habitats in the region except marshes. These adaptable birds become tame in cities but remain extremely shy in remote habitats. Robins feed on worms, insects, and fruits (cherries, apples, mountain ash, and cotoneaster). They spend the winter in large, social flocks. After arriving on the nesting grounds, the male immediately begins to establish a territory of about 1/3 acre, using a variety of displays to displace other males.

In contrast to virtually all of the other perching birds, robins do not seem to have well-defined courtship displays. Songs are uttered at dawn and dusk, but are most frequent just before the young hatch and do not seem to be related to courtship.

Robins are early nesters, often starting the first nest in April. The male brings most of the nesting material and the female places it and forms the nest by sitting in it and pressing her breast against the edges. This often leaves the female with a "mud-line" across her breast.

The sturdy, grass-lined nest is usually located in the crotch or horizontal limb of a tree and contains up to six light turquoise blue eggs. The young grow quickly. By the time they fledge, they closely resemble adults except for their densely spotted breasts. Immediately after the first brood leaves the nest, the adults build another nest and raise a second, and sometime a third, brood. In many instances, the male feeds the fledglings while the female starts a new nest.

―――SIMILAR SPECIES―――

Townsend's Solitaire
Myadestes townsendi

FIELD MARKS: 9 inches. Slim; white eye ring; gray plumage; pale salmon wing patches; long white tail; quiet, shy behavior.

STATUS: Ranges across western North America; in this region, found only in the BH and possibly the pine forests of western NE.

In May and June, look for Townsend's Solitaires perched on the outer or topmost branches of small trees along the edges of small clearings in open pine and fir or juniper forests. From these perches, they hawk insects like flycatchers. Townsend's Solitaires sing their beautiful song—a long series of loud, rapidly warbled, clear notes—from the tops of tall trees or while hovering in flight. Unlike many other songbirds, solitaires will actively defend winter feeding territories where their preferred berry crops are abundant.

American Robin

Townsend's Solitaire at nest

STARLINGS

European Starling
Sturnus vulgaris

FIELD MARKS: 8 inches. Plump; glossy black, iridescent plumage; long yellow bill; short tail; walks with a waddle. ***Winter:*** spotted plumage; dark bill.

STATUS: Introduced; now ranges all across North America; common permanent resident in much of the region; not found in the upper elevations of the BH; uncommon in BLNP.

European Starlings were brought to New York from Europe by a man who wanted to introduce to North America all the birds mentioned by Shakespeare. Far from musical, their seemingly ceaseless calls and squabbling consist of various squeaks, chirps, and whistles; they are also accomplished mimics and often mix snippets of other bird songs into their own. They have proliferated and displaced other more colorful and tamer birds, such as bluebirds and swallows, from nesting cavities, earning them the disdain of modern birders. Still, starlings are interesting birds.

Very adaptable, European Starlings inhabit relatively open habitats with crevices or cavities suitable for nesting—cities and short-grass farmlands are among their favorites. Their stout, straight bills and large, strong feet and legs are ideally suited to a bird that feeds on virtually anything it can locate while walking on the ground—insects, cherries, and seeds. They also are adept at locating suet and seeds offered at feeders.

In spring, the males usually arrive on the nesting grounds before the females. The males choose nest sites, which may be very close to one another, and begin defending them against other males, and, at the same time, attracting females. They do this by crowing, which they do by tilting their head up, fluffing out their throat feathers, and uttering a chortle of calls. When a female approaches, the male adds *"wing waving"* in the hope of attracting her to the nest site, along with *"bill wiping," "fluffing,"* and *"wing flicking."* He may also carry nest material in and out of the nesting cavity in front of her.

The female eventually chooses a male. Once paired, the two birds feed, perch, and roost together. She cleans out the nesting material that he had brought in, brings in grass of her own choosing, and lays her four to five bluish white eggs. The male assists the female during the incubation, but she usually takes the night shift. The young hatch in about twelve days and fledge about three weeks later. The adults may feed them for about a week after they leave the nest, but the juveniles soon leave to join other young starlings in huge flocks.

European Starling

Fledgling European Starlings

WAXWINGS

Cedar Waxwing
Bombycilla cedrorum

FIELD MARKS: 7 inches. Pale brown back, fading to yellowish on the breast; white undertail; black mask; **brown crest;** red waxy tips on wing coverts; yellow-tipped tail.

STATUS: Ranges all across the northern U.S.; fairly common summer breeder throughout ND, eastern SD, and the Missouri River valley in NE; occurs in the lower elevations of the BH.

HOT SPOTS: J. Clark Salyer NWR, ND; Waubay NWR and the Black Hills, SD; DeSoto NWR, NE.

Cedar Waxwings are gregarious birds that perch, feed, and fly in flocks most of the year. They have prominent crests and soft, silky plumage in subdued colors. The name "waxwing" refers to the waxy tips on the wing coverts. Their short, stout bills are adapted for eating fruit; sturdy legs and feet allow them to stretch in all directions to reach their meals.

Cedar Waxwings court by passing a berry or petal back and forth. The male may "side-hop" to the female and give her a berry. She takes the berry, hops away, then hops back and gives it to him. He takes the berry, hops away, and then hops back and returns it to her. The display ends when one of the pair eats the berry.

The nest is built between 4 and 50 feet above the ground in a conifer or deciduous bush. The male has a guarding perch nearby from which he watches for intruders and warns the female if danger approaches. Because the territory is not used to protect a food source, pairs may nest within 25 feet of each other with no conflict.

Waxwings nest later than most birds, so their young hatch about the time there are ripe berries and fruit available. For the first couple days, the helpless young eat a protein-rich diet of insects before switching to berries and fruit. The young become independent in about ten days and the family group begins to wander. In late summer, family groups may be seen around beaver ponds or similar areas, where they hawk insects from a conspicuous perch like flycatchers.

———SIMILAR SPECIES———

Bohemian Waxwing
Bombycilla garrulus

FIELD MARKS: 8 inches. Pale gray plumage; black mask; **crest; red, waxy tips on wing coverts;** yellow and **white spots on wings;** chestnut undertail coverts.

STATUS: Breeds in northern Canada and Alaska; erratic winter visitor in this region; sometimes in very large flocks.

Bohemian Waxwings are larger, grayer, and have a more northern distribution than Cedar Waxwings. Like their cousins, they are nomadic in winter and travel erratically in search of plentiful supplies of berries, sometimes wandering far south of their normal range.

Cedar Waxwing

Bohemian Waxwing

WARBLERS

Yellow Warbler *Dendroica petechia*

FIELD MARKS: 5 inches. *Male:* bright yellow plumage; rusty streaks on breast. *Female:* yellow green plumage.

STATUS: Common summer resident throughout the region.

The best-known and most widely distributed warbler, Yellow Warblers inhabit streamside thickets of willow, alder, and cottonwood. With slender, pointed bills they pick insects and larvae from trees and shrubs.

Excellent songsters and intensely territorial, the males defend their turf by singing their thin, wiry songs from prominent perches. The female builds her cup-shaped nest in a vertical crotch of a bush or tree, sometimes as high as 60 feet above the ground. She lays three to six eggs. After they hatch in ten to twelve days the male helps her feed the growing youngsters. Brown-headed Cowbirds (see pp. 198–99) often parasitize Yellow Warblers by laying eggs in the warbler's nest. If the warbler discovers the addition, it may construct a new floor over the cowbird egg and begin a new clutch.

Like most warblers, Yellow Warblers migrate to Mexico and South America in winter. The continuing destruction of habitat in their wintering grounds poses a serious threat to these birds.

——SIMILAR SPECIES——

Yellow-rumped Warbler *Dendroica coronata*

FIELD MARKS: 5 inches. *Male:* dark gray plumage; yellow patches on crown, throat, sides, and rump; white wing patches. *Female:* grayish brown plumage.

STATUS: Regular migrant throughout the region; common summer resident in the BH and BLNP.

Yellow-rumped Warblers inhabit mixed woods and usually nest in the top of a conifer. They are in almost constant motion—darting, flitting, hanging upside down, and hawking insects. The ranges of the two varieties meet in this region. The Audubon's Warbler, distinguishable by its yellow throat, breeds further west. The Myrtle Warbler, with a white throat and less white in its wings, nests farther north in central to northern Canada and Alaska, but is a regular migrant through this region.

Common Yellowthroat *Geothlypis trichas*

FIELD MARKS: 5 inches. Small; olive brown above; yellow throat. *Male:* black mask.

STATUS: Common summer resident throughout the region.

The Common Yellowthroat is a shy inhabitant of thick, damp shrubbery, marshes, and brushy undergrowth, usually near open water, and is most easily detected by its song. The male regularly sings while searching for small grasshoppers, beetles, moths, and other insects, but also periodically ascends to the uppermost branches of favored shrubs to proclaim his territory, calling "*witchety, witchety.*"

Yellow Warbler in hawthorn tree

Male Yellow-rumped Warbler

Male Common Yellowthroat

TANAGERS

Western Tanager   *Piranga ludoviciana*

FIELD MARKS: 7 inches. Stout bill. ***Male:* black and yellow plumage; orange red head;** black wings and tail; one yellow and one white wing bar. ***Female:*** yellow gray plumage; gray back; two thick wing bars.

STATUS: Fairly common summer resident in the BH and Pine Ridge areas; rare in BLNP.

In this region, these summer visitors are found only in the open conifer, mixed spruce-fir, lodgepole pine, and Douglas-fir–aspen habitats of the Black Hills and Pine Ridge. The males have brilliantly colored plumage, and both sexes sport stout bills. They are monogamous, and most sing either weak songs or no songs at all. Western Tanagers quietly search treetops for caterpillars and insects, and may dart out from high limbs to catch flying insects. They also eat fruit and nectar, and can sometimes be attracted to backyard feeders with dried fruit and oranges.

Tanagers typically place their shallow, saucerlike nest in a fork near the end of a branch midway up an evergreen tree. The male does not incubate but does help feed the young. The Western Tanager's casual song and *"pick-a-tuck"* call, drifting down from the treetops, are common sounds in the Black Hills and the easiest way to detect the bird's presence.

With the approach of winter Western Tanagers migrate to Mexico and Costa Rica.

——SIMILAR SPECIES——

Scarlet Tanager   *Piranga olivacea*

FIELD MARKS: 7 inches. ***Male:*** Red with **black wings and tail.** ***Female:*** Yellow green with **dark wings and tail.**

STATUS: Ranges throughout eastern U.S.; extends along river bottoms into central ND, SD, and NE; not found in the BH or BLNP. Rare to accidental migrant in western portions of the region.

In this area the gorgeous Scarlet Tanager is primarily limited to the forested slopes and valleys associated with river bottom forests. It arrives late in the spring, often after the trees are leafing out, and forages high in the forest canopy, so relatively little is known about its habits. Nests are rather loosely constructed and usually located high (35 to 50 feet) in the canopy on a horizontal limb. From limited observations, it appears as if the females do most of the work associated with incubating the eggs and raising the young.

Male Western Tanager

Scarlet Tanager —© Brian E. Small/www.briansmallphoto.com

SPARROWS

Chipping Sparrow
Spizella passerina

FIELD MARKS: 5 inches. **Solid rufous crown; "white eyebrow";** black eye line; **gray rump;** unstreaked gray below.

STATUS: Common summer resident throughout the region, including the BH; uncommon in BLNP. Currently populations appear to be declining.

Chipping Sparrows prefer open areas in dry environments with thinly scattered trees. Tolerant of human activity, they can also be found in parks, gardens, and backyards in residential areas.

This species gets its name from its song—an extended series of rapid, almost musical *"chips"*—which is usually delivered from the outermost branches of a tree. The male uses the song to establish his territory and attract females.

The nests are hair-lined cups on conifer branches, usually less than 10 feet above the ground. The female builds the nest but the male may accompany her on many of her trips to and from the nest. She lays three or four pale blue eggs and incubates them alone. They hatch after eleven or twelve days. The female broods the young for the first six or seven days after hatching and the male brings food for the female and the chicks. The young fledge in about ten days, but continue to be fed by the parents for another three or four weeks. Chipping Sparrows usually raise two broods each year.

Chipping Sparrows feed on seeds and insects they find on or near the ground. They can readily be attracted to feeders by millet seed.

——SIMILAR SPECIES——

Lark Sparrow
Chondestes grammacus

FIELD MARKS: 6 inches. Streaked brown above; **bold rufous, white, and black head pattern;** black central tail feathers; white corner and outer tail feathers.

STATUS: Fairly common summer resident in grassland habitats throughout the western part of the region except for parts of central ND; less common in the east and in the upper parts of the BH; common in BLNP.

Look for this boldly colored sparrow in dry, open woodlands and tall shrublands. Males often sing from exposed perches 8 to 12 feet high in a lone cottonwood or at the edge of the woods. One of our finest singers, the Lark Sparrow's song is a series of long, liquid trills and phrases.

The Lark Sparrow conceals its nest in dense vegetation on the ground. Nests are frequently parasitized by cowbirds (see pp. 198–99).

During migration, Lark Sparrows gather in large flocks in weedy fields and along roadsides, where they search for insects and seeds.

Chipping Sparrow

Lark Sparrow

Savannah Sparrow *Passerculus sandwichensis*

FIELD MARKS: 6 inches. Brown streaked plumage; **narrow, yellow eyebrow; short, notched tail.**

STATUS: Fairly common summer resident throughout the northern and western part of region; migrant only in most of NE; uncommon in lower elevations of the BH; common in BLNP.

Throughout spring the Savannah Sparrow sings its weak, lisping song from a prominent perch. Not as secretive as some of the other grassland sparrows, Savannah Sparrows are not difficult to spot. They build their nests in grass-lined hollows in short grass or sparse vegetation, such as the fringe of a marsh. Three or four eggs are laid in late May or June and incubated by the female. Both parents help feed the chicks, and fledging occurs in about ten days. The youngsters continue to be fed by the parents for about two weeks.

Depending on the season, Savannah Sparrows eat insects or seeds. In winter, they move mostly south of this region to avoid the snow.

——SIMILAR SPECIES——

Grasshopper Sparrow *Ammodramus savannarum*

FIELD MARKS: 5 inches. Heavily streaked brown plumage; **rufous spots on back;** unmarked, buffy breast; large bill; flat head; complete eye ring; pale, buffy face with dark "ear spot"; **short tail.**

STATUS: Ranges throughout the prairies of the Midwest and eastern U.S.; found in suitable habitats throughout this region; uncommon in the BH; abundant in BLNP.

Grasshopper Sparrows prefer mixed-grass prairies. From the top of a tall weed or bush or from a fence wire, they advertise their presence by singing their buzzy "grasshopper" song and utilizing their wing-flick display. When disturbed the female often does a "rodent run" rather than flying directly from the nest.

Song Sparrow *Melospiza melodia*

FIELD MARKS: 6 inches. Heavily streaked brown plumage; gray and brown striped head and face; **large central breast spot.**

STATUS: Common resident north of the SD-NE border; less common south into NE; common summer resident in the BH; uncommon in BLNP.

One of the first birds of spring, Song Sparrows arrive before the snow melts; some winter here. Tolerant of humans, they prefer the cover of shrubbery, hedgerows, brushlands, and forest edges, where they feed on the ground, scratching with both feet at once. With their cheerful and persistent singing, rich and varied repertoire of songs, and local and regional dialects they are aptly named.

The nest is usually low to the ground, well hidden in a tangle of brush. Song Sparrows usually lay four eggs and may have as many as three broods. They are commonly parasitized by cowbirds.

Savannah Sparrow

Grasshopper Sparrow
—Photo by Tom J. Ulrich

Song Sparrow

Dark-eyed Junco
Junco hyemalis

FIELD MARKS: 6 inches. Light pink bill; **dark eyes; gray or black head;** white belly; **white tail feathers flash in flight.**

White-winged race: uniform medium gray above and on breast; **white wing bars;** extensive white on outer 4 tail feathers; dark lores between eyes and bill.

Slate-colored race: **uniform dark gray above and on breast.**

Oregon race: **black hood;** brown back; **pinkish sides.**

Pink-sided race: **gray hood;** dull brown back; **extensive pinkish flanks;** dark lores.

Gray-headed race: gray upperparts; black lores; **rufous mantle;** light gray flanks.

STATUS: Common migrant throughout the region; White-winged is common resident in the BH, in BLNP, and in the Pine Ridge area of NE.

The Dark-eyed Juncos include several distinctly colored races that were once considered separate species. The White-winged variety is the common breeding junco in the Black Hills. Four other varieties migrate through this area.

Highly adaptable, Dark-eyed Juncos inhabit open conifer and aspen-conifer stands with grassy undergrowth. They hop around on the ground picking seeds and insects off the surface, rather than scratching as many sparrows do.

The female builds a simple grass nest on the ground, often on a steep slope, and frequently under the shelter of a tree, rock, or fallen log. She does the incubating. The male helps feed the young until they fledge and for a short time afterward. Two broods in a single season are common. Intruders face agitated adults who flit nearby, uttering a constant barrage of alarm calls.

As winter approaches, Dark-eyed Juncos move to the lowlands and tend to return to the same wintering areas each year. You can attract them to feeders stocked with millet or other small seeds, and may see several races together. Juncos move about in stable flocks with a well-established dominance hierarchy, where males usually dominate females and older birds dominate younger birds. Dominant birds displace subordinate birds with pecking attacks or by lunging. Birds close to each other in the hierarchy may face off, throwing their heads up and down in a "head-dance" display. If neither bird backs down, they may rise three or four feet into the air clawing furiously at each other. Rarely do these disputes extend beyond one or two clawing matches before the two birds simply go back to feeding—although not adjacent to each other.

Dark-eyed Junco (Oregon)

Dark-eyed Junco (Pink-sided)

Dark-eyed Junco (Slate-colored)

CARDINALS AND GROSBEAKS

Northern Cardinal   *Cardinalis cardinalis*

FIELD MARKS: 9 inches. **Crest.** *Male:* **red overall;** large red bill; black lores and throat. *Female:* reddish brown overall; **black face; red-orange bill;** reddish tint to wings and tail.

STATUS: Ranges across eastern U.S.; extends into this region in the Red River Valley of southeastern ND, along the Missouri River valley of eastern SD, and across most of NE east of the Sandhills area; rare in the BH; not recorded in BLNP.

This large, striking red bird lives along forest edges or brushy forest habitats with numerous openings. It also frequents residential areas with the right mix of trees, brush, and open areas. Its beautiful song, striking appearance, and tolerance of human neighbors has made it well liked—so much so that seven states have made it their state bird, and it is the mascot for numerous schools and sports teams.

Northern Cardinals forage by hopping about on the ground or moving through shrubbery and trees. They eat insects, spiders, snails, slugs, fruit, and weed seeds. Waste grain, blossoms, buds, and sap from the sap wells drilled by sapsuckers are also consumed. They can be attracted to feeders by sunflower seeds and cracked corn.

In winter many cardinals, especially the juveniles, move about in flocks, frequenting areas where food is plentiful. They keep in contact with chip-calls, feeding and roosting together. In late February the flocks begin to break up and the birds disperse to find territories.

Pair-bonding in cardinals is fairly permanent. In cases where a pair has stayed on their territory throughout the winter, they can be observed beginning to feed together as the breeding season approaches.

Soon after the pair forms they begin courtship singing. Northern Cardinals are one of the few birds in which both sexes are equally adept at singing. The two birds, often perched some distance apart on the territory, begin "countersinging." One of the birds sings a song (a series of melodic and piercing whistles), which is then copied by the other. Each bird sings in turn until one changes the phrasing; the other bird mimics the change and the singing continues.

Cardinals are highly territorial, and males expel intruders by chasing. If a pair of cardinals intrudes on the territory, the resident male chases the intruding male and the female chases the intruding female.

Northern Cardinals raise two or three, and sometimes even four, broods each summer. By May or June, the female is busy building nests, incubating, and, with the help of the male, feeding young. Although the nest may be very close to human activities, it is usually well hidden in dense vegetation.

Male Northern Cardinal —Photo by Tom J. Ulrich

Black-headed Grosbeak   *Pheucticus melanocephalus*

FIELD MARKS: 8 inches. *Male:* stout, light-colored bill; black head; orange neck and breast; yellow central belly; orange rump; black back and wings with white markings. *Female:* buff and brown instead of black and orange; striped head; finely streaked flanks.

STATUS: Ranges primarily west of this region; extends east through the western two-thirds of ND, SD, and NE; not present in the upper BH; uncommon in BLNP.

Grosbeaks are easily recognized by their oversized, conical bills. Their bills are pointed at the tip for picking up seeds and heavy at the base for cracking them open. Fairly tolerant of humans, they are easily attracted to feeders that offer sunflower seeds. They are also brightly colored and have beautiful songs, which they proclaim from prominent perches during spring. These characteristics make them fairly easy to observe and well liked by birders.

Male Black-headed Grosbeaks usually arrive about a week before the females. They scatter through a broad range of open habitats—riparian woodlands, second-growth forests, forest edges, orchards, and suburbs—and sing to claim their territories. When the females arrive the males seem to spend the first few days chasing them off. They soon begin to tolerate the females in the territory.

In June or July, the females build loose, poorly constructed nests in the outer branches of trees or shrubs near forest openings, and deposit three or four eggs. The nest is usually less than 10 feet above the ground and, according to one South Dakota study, often found in box elder trees. Incubation takes from twelve to fourteen days and is shared by both birds. Grosbeak males assist the females in raising the young much more than most birds.

Black-headed Grosbeaks hunt caterpillars, grasshoppers, bees, wasps, and other insects. Ripe berries and other fruits supplement their diets seasonally. They winter in Mexico and Central and South America.

——SIMILAR SPECIES——

Rose-breasted Grosbeak   *Pheucticus ludovicianus*

FIELD MARKS: 8 inches. *Male:* black head, back, wings, and tail; **rose breast;** white belly; white wing bars; heavy bill. *Female:* streaked brown plumage above; **boldly striped head; heavy, pale bill;** streaked whitish breast.

STATUS: Ranges across northeastern U.S.; fairly common breeder in eastern parts of ND, SD, and NE; rare in the BH, BLNP, and western portions of this region.

Although very different in color, the beautiful Rose-breasted Grosbeak is similar to the Black-headed Grosbeak in breeding behavior. Where their ranges overlap, these two species hybridize to some degree. Sightings of Rose-breasted Grosbeaks have increased in the western portion of the region in recent years.

Male Black-headed Grosbeak

Male Rose-breasted Grosbeak —Photo by Tom J. Ulrich

BLACKBIRDS AND ORIOLES

Bobolink
Dolichonyx oryzivorus

FIELD MARKS: 7 inches. *Male:* primarily black, including the breast; **light yellow nape; white rump and scapulars.** *Female:* streaked brown above; pale nape; lightly streaked flanks; buffy breast.

STATUS: Ranges across the northern half of the U.S.; fairly common breeder in suitable habitats throughout the region; rare in the BH and in BLNP.

Bobolinks are conspicuous residents of the tall-grass prairie regions. The males are easily seen singing from a tall weed, fence post, or shrub near wet meadows, hayfields, and mixed-grass habitats. They arrive on the nesting grounds a week or so ahead of the females. You can observe adjacent males do their parallel flight or walk displays along the borders of their territories. When the females arrive, they spread out across the habitat, beginning with one female per male. Eventually as many as four females may be found on a single territory.

Males sing their unique, banjolike song from prominent perches, and also use song-flights. The displays often show off the highly visible yellow nape, which apparently plays a role in both territorial defense and courtship.

Once the business of nest building, incubation, and feeding the young begins, the males become surprisingly tolerant of other Bobolink males and allow them to venture relatively near the nest sites. At the same time, they are surprisingly aggressive toward other species.

The female builds a ground nest and incubates the single brood of four to five eggs for about thirteen days. The male helps feed the chicks to some extent, and two weeks after hatching, the young fledge and disperse into the surrounding grasses.

Bobolinks require tall-grass habitats for nesting and are being affected by a continual loss of those habitats. Hayfields can offer a substitute, but unfortunately mowing often coincides with fledging, resulting in greatly reduced breeding success.

——SIMILAR SPECIES——

Lark Bunting
Calamospiza melanocorys

FIELD MARKS: 7 inches. *Male:* **black body; white wing patches.** *Female:* streaked brown plumage; brown cheek patch; **pale wing patches.**

STATUS: Fairly common breeder throughout region except extreme northeastern ND and extreme southeastern NE; not found in the BH; abundant in BLNP.

Lark Buntings inhabit the short- and mixed-grass prairies and plains, preferring sparser habitats than Bobolinks. The polygamous males return year after year to the same territories and try to attract females by flying up in the air a few yards and then uttering their songs while slowly circling back to the ground on uptilted wings.

Male Bobolink

Male Lark Bunting

Red-winged Blackbird *Agelaius phoeniceus*

FIELD MARKS: 9 inches. Sharply pointed bill. *Male:* black plumage; **scarlet wing patch with yellow lower border.** *Female:* heavily streaked brown plumage; reddish tint on shoulder.

STATUS: Abundant summer resident throughout the region, including the BH and BLNP; may winter in flocks at feedlots, especially in the southern portions of the region.

Highly visible and very vocal, Red-winged Blackbirds are easily seen perched on fence posts or on tall reeds and cattails. Their strong, pointed bills enable them to eat a wide variety of food, including insects, seeds, grains, and berries.

Among the first migrant passerines to return to the region in the spring, the Red-winged Blackbird's arrival is a sure sign that warmer weather is on its way. The males return to this region as early as February and set up territories in the cattails or along wet borders. Their loud, distinctive *"oak-a-leeee-o"* call is very hard to miss.

Several females may nest in the territory of a single male. The females suspend loosely woven cups in clumps of last year's cattails and line the nests with fine grasses. Although they traditionally nested only in marshes, Red-winged Blackbirds are beginning to colonize grassy fields away from water. Corn, grain, fruit, and weed seeds provide nutrition during most of the year except for the breeding season, when the chicks are fed insects. After raising the young, the adults stay in the marshes while they molt their tail feathers. As fall approaches, these birds typically gather in mixed flocks with other blackbirds and starlings. Some winter in this region, but most fly south.

——SIMILAR SPECIES——

Yellow-headed Blackbird *Xanthocephalus xanthocephalus*

FIELD MARKS: 10 inches. *Male:* black body; **yellow head, neck, and chest;** large white wing patches visible in flight. *Female:* dark grayish brown plumage; pale yellow throat and chest.

STATUS: Abundant summer resident throughout the region except the higher elevations of the BH.

Yellow-headed Blackbirds arrive about a month after their red-winged cousins. As with the Red-wings, the males arrive first to set up their territories, often displacing red-winged Blackbirds that arrived earlier. The Yellow-headed Blackbird's song is harsh and unmusical, something like the creaking of a rusty gate.

When the females arrive, they choose a nest site and mate with the male who "owns" that territory. Where Yellow-headed and Red-winged Blackbirds share the same marsh, they tend to nest in distinct colonies. Yellow-headed Blackbirds usually occupy the cattails and reeds in deeper water. The red-wings nest in shallower water.

Male Red-winged Blackbird

Female Red-winged Blackbird

Male Yellow-headed Blackbird

Western Meadowlark
Sturnella neglecta

FIELD MARKS: 9 inches. Plump profile; streaked brown plumage; long, pointed bill; **yellow malar;** yellow breast with black V-shaped neckband; **whitish flanks;** short tail with white outer tail feathers; tail flicks almost constantly.

STATUS: Common to abundant summer resident throughout the region.

The Western Meadowlark inhabits open grasslands and pastures. Watch for males proclaiming their territorial rights in early spring while perched on posts or wires, singing their beautiful, exuberant, liquid song. They also utilize a "jump-flight" display in which they flutter into the air with their wings held high and their legs hanging down. Often, this display is seen at territorial borders and a jump-flight by one bird is followed quickly by one from the other.

The females arrive on the nesting grounds two to four weeks after the males. After the customary courtship displays, two or even three females may build their nests in the territory of one male. The grass nests are built on the ground in surprisingly short vegetation and camouflaged by weaving an overhanging dome from nearby grasses.

Average clutch size is five, with the female building the nest and doing all the incubation. The male helps feed the young a diet of insects and seeds. The adults continue to feed the young for about a month after they leave the nest.

Following the breeding season, meadowlarks form large flocks (20 to 300 birds) and forage in croplands on waste grain and weed seeds. At night, they take shelter in the tall grass of marshes. They head south in September or October to winter along the Gulf Coast, although flocks can often be seen further inland.

As houses replace the open grasslands they require, meadowlarks disappear, creating concern about their future.

——SIMILAR SPECIES——

Eastern Meadowlark
Sturnella magna

FIELD MARKS: 9 inches. Plump profile; streaked brown plumage; long, pointed bill; bold head pattern with dark head-stripe; **white malar;** yellow breast; **buffy flanks;** black neck band; short tail with white outer tail feathers; tail flicks almost constantly.

STATUS: Ranges primarily east of this region, but extends into southeastern NE.

The habitats and habits of Eastern Meadowlarks are very similar to those of the western. Only subtle differences in their plumage and songs allow us to distinguish between the two. In areas of range overlap, the Eastern Meadowlark is found in the lower, moister habitats, leaving the drier sites to the Western Meadowlark.

Western Meadowlark

Eastern Meadowlark —Photo by Vernon Eugene Grove Jr.

Brown-headed Cowbird   *Molothrus ater*

FIELD MARKS: 7 inches. **Short, conical bill;** stubby tail. *Male:* black body; **brown head.** *Female:* gray brown plumage.

STATUS: Fairly common summer resident throughout the region.

Brown-headed Cowbirds inhabit woodland edges, creek bottoms, brushy thickets, and agricultural lands. They historically followed bison herds, and now are often seen following grazing cattle or horses to feed on grasshoppers and other insects that the moving animals stir up.

Cowbirds are the only species of bird in North America that are solely brood parasites. They do not raise their own young, instead laying their eggs in the nests of other species for the foster parents to raise.

Male cowbirds hang out together while the females wander the countryside in search of suitable nests in which to lay their eggs. They locate nests by sitting on a high perch or moving quietly through thick underbrush and observing the bird activity around them. They may also fly into a bush or shrub and make a lot of racket, hoping to flush a bird from her nest.

When a female finds a nest, she mates with one of the males from a nearby flock. She enters her chosen nest in the morning when the host is away. If the nest already contains eggs, she may roll one out and replace it with her own. In other cases, she simply lays her egg and leaves. A female may lay around forty eggs per year in different nests, of which two or three may reach maturity.

Warblers, vireos, flycatchers, and finches are the most common hosts, but cowbird eggs have been found in the nests of over 150 different species. The hosts may puncture the egg and throw it out, as robins and catbirds sometimes do. They may either desert the nest or build another layer of nest material over the cowbird egg, as Yellow Warblers and phoebes are known to do. Or they may simply accept the extra egg and raise the resulting young as their own.

Cowbird eggs hatch in ten days, usually before those of the host. The young cowbird grows quickly and often outcompetes the rightful nestlings. Still, their reputation of being extremely detrimental to other species may be overstated, as studies have shown that nests from which a cowbird was successfully fledged also fledged youngsters of the host species. The presence of a cowbird egg reduced the nesting success of the host species by one chick. However, there are instances, particularly in host species that are already endangered, in which the reduction of a clutch by even a single fledgling is critical.

Male Brown-headed Cowbird

Female Brown-headed Cowbird

Common Grackle
Quiscalus quiscula

FIELD MARKS: 12 inches. Pale yellow eyes. *Male:* glossy brown black body; head with blue, green, or violet iridescence; long, heavy, pointed bill; **long, wedge-shaped tail.** *Female:* dull gray brown plumage. *Young:* brown eyes until October.

STATUS: Common summer resident throughout much of the region, including the lower BH and BLNP.

Common Grackles inhabit open country near water and residential areas: parks, farmsteads, windbreaks. These omnivorous blackbirds feed on insects, seeds, and nuts, as well as human refuse.

The males arrive in the region before the females. When the females arrive, courtship flights—a female with five or six males in hot pursuit—are common. The nest is a bulky cup-shaped structure hidden on a horizontal branch of an evergreen, and a number of Common Grackle nests are often grouped into loose colonies. The female selects the nest site, gathers nesting materials, builds the nest, and incubates the three to six eggs. The role of the male in this process is to defend a small area of the nesting tree immediately surrounding the nest and to help feed the young.

The din that huge groups of these noisy birds create as they communally roost in large stands of trees, and the resulting volume of droppings are often unappreciated by nearby human residents. The song is merely a rusty squawk.

During migration, Common Grackles are often found in large mixed flocks with Brown-headed Cowbirds, Red-winged Blackbirds, and European Starlings.

——SIMILAR SPECIES——

Brewer's Blackbird
Euphagus cyanocephalus

FIELD MARKS: 9 inches. Sharply pointed bill. *Male:* iridescent black plumage; purplish gloss on head; greenish gloss on body; **whitish eyes.** *Female:* grayish brown plumage; dark eyes.

STATUS: Fairly common to common summer resident throughout the region and in the BH.

Once strictly a bird of the western United States, the Brewer's Blackbird is extending its range across the Great Plains. A dryland species, it forages on the ground for insects and seeds. As it walks, it jerks its head in a very characteristic manner. In migration, it is often found in mixed flocks with other blackbird species.

Male Common Grackle

Male Brewer's Blackbird

Baltimore Oriole
Icterus galbula

FIELD MARKS: 8 inches. White wing bars. *Male:* long, pointed bill; **black head, throat, and upper back; orange sides, belly, and rump;** black wings with **orange shoulder patch.** *Female:* yellowish gray plumage; dark wings.

STATUS: Ranges from the Atlantic Coast through the western limits of this region; fairly common local summer resident throughout most of region; less so in the BH and in central MT; rare in BLNP.

Although they spend much of their time high in treetops where they search for insects, these colorful birds are a welcome addition to any neighborhood. Just a glimpse of them brightens a day. They have a beautiful, flutelike, warbling song and the females are also excellent songsters.

Male Baltimore Orioles arrive on the nesting grounds and set up their territories. The females arrive a short time later and, after an appropriate period of courting with songs and displays, choose a mate. Countersinging (see Northern Cardinal, p. 188) is also practiced by orioles. The female begins gathering fibers from old milkweed stalks or similar fibers and weaving them into a nest. Nests often contain string, yarn, tarp fibers, bailing twine, and other man-made materials. Hung high in the air (often at least 25 feet) and located almost on the tips of the branches, the sac-shaped nest is in almost constant motion from even the slightest breeze. Both the Baltimore and Bullock's Orioles weave nests that are deeper than wide and may have a lateral rather than a top opening.

Orioles can be attracted to feeders that offer fruit and sugar water. In fall, they begin moving to South America, where they spend the winter.

——SIMILAR SPECIES——

Bullock's Oriole
Icterus bullockii

FIELD MARKS: 9 inches. *Male:* long, pointed bill; **black cap, eye line,** throat, and back; **orange cheeks, sides, belly, and rump;** black wings with **white shoulder patches.** *Female:* yellowish gray plumage; dark wings with white wing bars.

STATUS: Ranges from the Pacific Coast east; fairly common summer resident in MT and the western third of ND, SD, and NE; common in the foothills of the BH; rare in BLNP.

Behavior and breeding habits are almost identical to those of the Baltimore variety. Once considered separate species, these birds were recently lumped together into one because of the occurrence of hybrids in areas where their ranges overlapped.

Orchard Oriole
Icterus spurius

FIELD MARKS: 7 inches. White wing bars. *Male:* long, pointed bill; **black head, throat and upper back; chestnut sides, belly, and rump;** black wings with **chestnut shoulder patches.** *Female:* yellowish gray plumage; dark wings.

STATUS: Ranges from the Atlantic Coast west; fairly common summer resident throughout most of this region; not common in the BH and in BLNP.

Habits are very similar to those of the other orioles, although this species is seen more frequently foraging in low shrubs. The nest of the Orchard Oriole is wider than deep, making it possible to distinguish from those of the other orioles.

Male Baltimore Oriole —Photo by Tom J. Ulrich

Male Bullock's Oriole
    —Photo by Tom J. Ulrich

Male Orchard Oriole

FINCHES

Cassin's Finch
Carpodacus cassinii

FIELD MARKS: 6 inches. Thin white eye ring; light, straight-edged bill; heavily streaked plumage. *Male:* **reddish wash on head and throat; light, unstreaked belly.** *Voice:* distinctive double or triple note call in flight.

STATUS: Fairly common resident in the BH; accidental elsewhere.

Cassin's Finches are one of the species whose range in this region is limited to the Black Hills. There, they are found in coniferous forests, preferring open, dry pine forests or forest edges.

During the spring breeding season, male Cassin's Finches sing a varied, liquid, warbling song. The female builds the cup-shaped nest high in a tree and well out toward the tip of a branch. She lays four or five eggs and incubates them herself. Both sexes feed the young.

Cassin's Finches forage in the tops of trees or on the ground, eating the seeds and buds of conifers. They have stout bills with an internal groove to hold a seed in place and large jaw muscles to help crush it. They use their tongues to peel and discard the husk. A powerful gizzard helps digest the seed. In summer, they add insects to their diet, as well as some fruits and berries. They often gather in flocks and forage away from the nest wherever they can find an abundance of seeds. They are attracted to bird feeders offering sunflower seeds and millet.

——SIMILAR SPECIES——

House Finch
Carpodacus mexicanus

FIELD MARKS: 5 inches. *Male:* **short, dark, stout bill;** streaked brown plumage; red forehead, eyebrow, and throat; **streaked sides.** *Female:* heavily streaked brown plumage.

STATUS: Extending its range into this region from both the east and the west; accidental in the BH.

House Finches prefer the lowlands of the region and commonly inhabit open woodlands and urban areas. They have adapted well to humans and have begun nesting in the abundant nooks and crannies of buildings. Males in some areas have a yellow wash on the forehead and breast instead of the usual red, possibly the result of differences in diet.

Purple Finch
Carpodacus purpureus

FIELD MARKS: 5 inches. *Male:* wine red head, throat, and breast; reddish wash on back and breast; notched tail. *Female:* **whitish "eyebrows"** and lower cheeks; mottled brown above, heavily streaked below; notched tail. *Voice:* distinctive, sharp, metallic *tick* uttered in flight.

STATUS: Irregular winter visitor throughout the region; accidental in the BH; not recorded in BLNP.

Purple Finches inhabit mixed forests, open woodlands, and suburbs. Primarily seed eaters, they also eat apple, birch, and aspen buds, insects, caterpillars, and various fruits.

Male Cassin's Finch
Inset: *Female Cassin's Finch*

Male House Finch

Male Purple Finch
—© Brian E. Small/www.briansmallphoto.com

Red Crossbill
Loxia curvirostra

FIELD MARKS: 6 inches. **Crossed mandibles; dark, unbarred wings.** *Male:* brick red plumage. *Female:* yellow to olive gray plumage.

STATUS: Irregular visitor throughout the region and in BLNP; regular breeder in the BH.

The Red Crossbill lives in spruce and pine forests with abundant cone crops. The unusual bill with its crossed tips is ideally suited to prying open spruce cones, and capable of opening pine and fir cones while the bird scoops out the seeds with its tongue. The crossbill dangles upside down to snip off a cone and carries it to a perch, holding it down with one foot while extracting the seeds. The Red Crossbill's bold and deliberate manner allows fortunate birders to closely observe this process.

Red Crossbills are unique in that they nest almost any time of year when sufficient conifer seeds are available—even when the days are short and snow blankets the ground. In this region, where they depend primarily on spruce seeds, they nest anytime between January and July, or possibly longer. Where pine seeds are available, they nest in the spring. In larch forests, they nest in late summer. In mixed spruce and pine forests, nesting may extend over ten months of the year. There is some thought that Red Crossbills might actually represent as many as six or seven species, each adapted to a specific coniferous tree species.

While most birds rely on insects to provide protein to their rapidly growing youngsters, crossbills raise their young exclusively on a diet of seeds. The adults gather large quantities of seeds in their gullets and return at infrequent intervals (twenty to sixty minutes) to the nest to regurgitate them.

When not breeding, they wander erratically, searching for abundant supplies of cones.

————SIMILAR SPECIES————

White-winged Crossbill
Loxia leucoptera

FIELD MARKS: 6 inches. **Crossed mandibles; white wing bars.** *Male:* bright pinkish red plumage; black wings. *Female:* olive gray plumage; dark wings.

STATUS: Irregular visitor throughout the region and in the BH; not recorded in BLNP.

White-winged Crossbills nest in northern forests from just south of the U.S.-Canadian border north to central Alaska. Except for favored nesting localities, these crossbills are found in this region only in winter. They normally venture only as far south as the Black Hills, but their wanderings may occasionally take them farther south.

Although they feed mostly on seeds and nest when this food is available, White-winged Crossbills also eat insects. They are attracted to big-game salt licks and salted highways. They will frequent bird feeders stocked with sunflower seeds.

Male Red Crossbill

Female Red Crossbill

Male White-winged Crossbill

American Goldfinch
Carduelis tristis

FIELD MARKS: 5 inches. **Black wings** with white wing bars; black tail. *Male:* **bright black and yellow plumage**; black forehead; yellow body. *Female:* greenish yellow color. *Call:* "Per-chic-er-re."

STATUS: Fairly common summer resident throughout most of region; not found in the upper BH; common in BLNP.

Throughout the winter and early spring, American Goldfinches travel about in small flocks. They may swarm bird feeders stocked with sunflower or thistle seeds. The sexes look similar at this time, but as spring approaches, the males begin to grow their bright black and yellow plumage.

Their tweezerlike bills are ideal for extracting the seeds from thistles, sunflowers, dandelions, and other composites. In fact, the American Goldfinch is believed to be the only bird capable of eating teasel seeds, which are located at the base of long, spiked tubes.

American Goldfinches often do not begin nest building until late July or August, so the hatching of their eggs coincides with the availability of thistle seeds. Their nests are located about 5 to 15 feet high in a cluster of upright branches or the fork of a limb. The nests are tightly woven of plant fibers and lined with thistle or cattail down. As a finishing touch, they may have spider webs bound around the rim. It has been reported that the nests are so tightly woven that they will hold water.

The four to five eggs are incubated by the female. When the young hatch, they are fed by both parents. Unlike most birds, which raise their young on insects, goldfinches feed their youngsters a regurgitated seed mixture, which they thrust down the throats of the nestlings.

After the nesting season, American Goldfinches once more gather in flocks to forage in open weedy fields and thickets.

——SIMILAR SPECIES——

Pine Siskin
Carduelis pinus

FIELD MARKS: 5 inches. Small size; thin, pointed bill; **heavily streaked brown above**; streaked white below; **yellow often visible in wings and at base of tail.**

STATUS: Common resident in the coniferous forests of the region and in the BH; uncommon in BLNP.

Noisy, gregarious, and nomadic, Pine Siskins fly in groups, uttering light twittering notes that seem to be synchronized with their wing beats. Like many finches, they wander erratically in winter, but are regulars—often with goldfinches—at feeders offering sunflower and thistle seeds. Their tame dispositions make them a joy to have around, as they may stay perched within a foot or two as you fill their feeder.

Male American Goldfinch

Female American Goldfinch

Pine Siskin

WEAVER FINCHES

House Sparrow
Passer domesticus

FIELD MARKS: 6 inches. *Male:* brown and gray plumage; black bill; gray crown; **black throat and upper breast**; white cheeks; **chestnut nape**; white wing bar. *Female:* gray brown plumage; gray below; pale "eyebrow."

STATUS: Abundant resident around developed areas throughout the region; absent from remote habitats in the BH; common in BLNP.

Weaver Finches are primarily an Old World family of birds. Named for the nest-weaving habits of some of its members—who weave the most complex and largest nests in the world—Weaver Finches have short, conical bills adapted to cracking seeds. Two introduced species represent this family in North America: the Eurasian Tree Sparrow and the House Sparrow. Only the House Sparrow is found in this region.

Introduced to Brooklyn, New York, in the 1850s, this native of Great Britain has flourished in the United States and Canada. Bold and impudent, yet cautious, these birds have since taken up residence wherever human construction leaves small cracks or crevices that provide access for nesting. Aggressive when competing for nest sites and food, they displace many native species, raising the ire of birders everywhere.

In spring and early summer, male House Sparrows locate a nesting site and then find a nearby perch from which to advertise that they are the owner of a nest site. They may sit and chirp repeatedly to attract a female. If a female approaches, the male will flutter to the nest site to entice her to nest there. Once a female accepts the site and a pair-bond is formed, the pair defends the site against other House Sparrows. The female defends against other females while the male takes care of other males.

Nest building consists of packing grass, paper, and feathers into the crevice to form a rather messy nest. Where crevices are not available, House Sparrows may construct round, dome-shaped nests in trees or shrubs. A clutch usually consists of four eggs, and the pair raises two or three broods each year. The female incubates and the male helps feed the hatchlings. The young fledge in fifteen to seventeen days and are fed by the adults away from the nest for about another week. Food for these noisy and gregarious birds is primarily seeds and whatever scraps they can find.

House Sparrows gather to sleep at large communal roosts at night and at smaller communal roosts during the day for resting and preening. There is speculation that the daytime roosts may have some function in communicating where food sources are located, but it may be just that—speculation.

Male House Sparrow

Female House Sparrow

DUCK WING — UPPER SURFACE

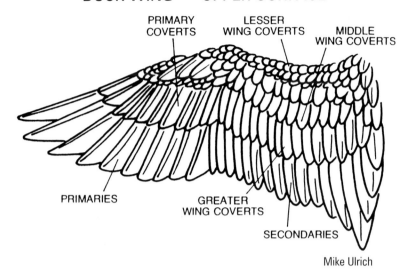

PRIMARY COVERTS

LESSER WING COVERTS

MIDDLE WING COVERTS

PRIMARIES

GREATER WING COVERTS

SECONDARIES

Mike Ulrich

PARTS OF A BIRD

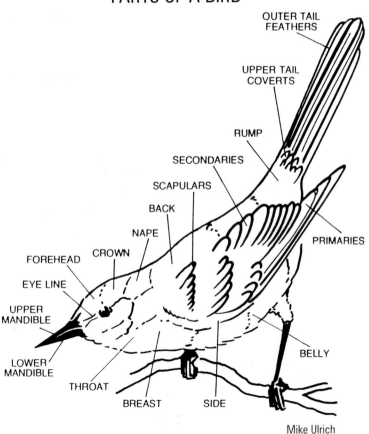

OUTER TAIL FEATHERS

UPPER TAIL COVERTS

RUMP

SECONDARIES

SCAPULARS

BACK

NAPE

CROWN

FOREHEAD

EYE LINE

UPPER MANDIBLE

PRIMARIES

LOWER MANDIBLE

BELLY

THROAT

BREAST

SIDE

Mike Ulrich

GLOSSARY

altricial. Describes young that hatch blind, naked, and helpless, thus needing longer-term care than young of other species. Contrast **precocial**.

brackish. Describes a mixture of fresh and salt water.

brood. The group of young birds that hatch from a single clutch of eggs. Also, to nestle with chicks to keep them warm.

cambium. The layer of soft, growing tissue between the bark and wood of trees and shrubs.

carrion. Dead and decaying flesh.

clutch. A group of eggs laid by one bird.

coniferous. Cone-bearing plants, in particular evergreen trees with needlelike leaves.

covert. See **wing covert**.

crest. A tuft of elongated feathers that extends backward from the top of the head.

crown. The top of the head.

deciduous. Refers to plants that drop their leaves each year.

dimorphic. Refers to a species in which the sexes differ in color or size; may also refer to a species that has two different color phases.

diurnal. Active during daylight hours. Contrast **nocturnal.**

eclipse plumage. A nondescript plumage that certain birds, such as male ducks, acquire at the end of the breeding season.

edge. Area where different habitat types meet, such as grassland meeting forest or sagebrush meeting grassland.

emergent vegetation. Aquatic plants that are rooted underwater and grow up out of the water, such as reeds and cattails.

fledge. To leave the nest; usually occurs after the young are fully feathered and able to fly.

foliage. The leaves of a tree or bush.

gallinaceous. Said of birds from the order Galliformes that resemble domestic fowl.

gizzard. A heavily muscled organ that aids digestion of hard seeds by mechanically grinding them.

gorget. Brilliant patch of feathers covering the throats of male hummingbirds.

gregarious. Said of birds that habitually associate with others in flocks.

gular. Relating to the throat.

hawking. Pursuing or attacking prey in flight.

horns. Tufts of feathers that extend upward from the sides of the head, as on some owls.

incubate. To keep eggs warm until they hatch.

iridescent. Shiny, almost metallic feather color that results from the diffraction of light rays and not from pigmentation; includes the gorgets of male hummingbirds.

larvae. Immature young of insects and invertebrates.

lek. Traditional site where male birds of certain species, such as Sharp-tailed Grouse, gather to perform courtship displays to attract females.

lore. The feathers between the eye and the bill.

malar. Relating to the cheekbone or the cheek.

molt. To shed and replace feathers; usually occurs after the breeding season and before the fall migration.

monogamous. Refers to a species that breeds with only one individual during a breeding cycle.

mustache. A strip of colored feathers that extends backward from the base of the bill.

nape. The back of the neck.

nictitating membrane. A clear inner eyelid that protects the eye during swift flight, underwater swimming, when flying through thick brush, etc.

nocturnal. Active during the night. Contrast **diurnal**.

nomadic. Wandering from place to place, seemingly without a pattern.

omnivorous. Eating both plants and animals for food.

plumage. The feathers of a bird.

polygamous. Refers to a species that breeds with more than one mate during a single breeding cycle.

precocial. Describes young that are well developed, covered with down, and able to leave the nest and run about soon after hatching. Contrast **altricial**.

prehensile. Capable of precise movement and adapted for grasping or holding by wrapping around.

primaries. The outermost and longest flight feathers of the wing.

raptor. A bird of prey, such as a hawk or eagle.

rump. The back portion of a bird just above the base of the tail feathers.

scapulars. The group of feathers on the shoulder of the bird, alongside the back.

secondaries. The innermost and shortest flight feathers of the wing. (See duck wing diagram on page 212.)

solitary. A bird that prefers to live alone and avoids the company of others of its species, except during the breeding season.

spatulate. Spoon shaped.

species. A group of animals or plants that exhibit common characteristics and can interbreed and produce fertile young.

speculum. The bright, often iridescent, patch of color on the wings of some birds, especially ducks.

stoop. A swift dive in pursuit of prey, characteristic of many raptors.

territory. A section of habitat that an individual or breeding pair actively defends.

thermal. A rising current of air that results from the unequal heating of the earth's surface; soaring birds commonly ride thermals to gain altitude or remain aloft with minimal effort.

tipping. A method of feeding in which ducks, geese, and swans "tip" their rumps in the air and reach below the surface of the water with their head and neck.

torpor. A state in which the metabolism drops to an extremely low level as a means of conserving energy.

wing coverts. Small feathers that overlap and cover the bases of the large flight feathers.

SUGGESTED REFERENCES

Bird Identification

Farrand, John Jr. *The Audubon Society Master Guide to Birding*. 3 vols. New York: Alfred A. Knopf, 1983.

Harrison, Hal H. *A Field Guide to Western Birds' Nests*. Boston: Houghton Mifflin, 2001.

Kaufman, Kenn. *Kaufman Field Guide to Birds of North America*. Boston: Houghton Mifflin, 2005.

National Geographic Field Guide to the Birds of North America, 4th edition. National Geographic Society, 2002.

Robbins, Chandler S., Bertel Bruun, and Herbert S. Zim. *Birds of North America: A Guide to Field Identification*. New York: Golden Guides from St. Martin's Press, 2001.

Sibley, David Allen. *The Sibley Guide to Birds*. New York: Alfred A. Knopf, 2000.

National Audubon Society Field Guide to North American Birds: Western Region. New York: Alfred A. Knopf, 1994.

Bird Behavior

Dennis, John V. *Beyond the Bird Feeder: The Habits and Behavior of Feeding-Station Birds When They Are Not at Your Feeder*. New York: Alfred A. Knopf, 1981.

Johnsgard, Paul A. *Birds of the Great Plains: Breeding Species and Their Distribution*. Lincoln: University of Nebraska Press, 1979.

Sibley, David Allen. *The Sibley Guide to Bird Life and Behavior*. New York: Alfred A Knopf, 2001.

Stokes, Donald W., and Lillian Q. Stokes. *Stokes Guide to Bird Behavior*. 3 vols. Boston: Little, Brown and Company, 1983.

Locating and Observing Birds

Brainerd, John W. *The Nature Observer's Handbook: Learning to Appreciate Our Natural World.* Chester, CT.: The Globe Pequot Press, 1986.

Butcher, Russell D. *America's National Wildlife Refuges: A Complete Guide.* Lanham, MD: Roberts Rinehart Publishers, 2003.

Fischer, Carol and Hank. *Montana Wildlife Viewing Guide.* Helena, MT: Falcon Press, 1995.

Gray, Mary T. *Colorado Wildlife Viewing Guide.* Helena, MT: Falcon Press, 1992.

Jones, John Oliver. *Where the Birds Are.* New York: William Morrow and Company, 1990.

Knue, Joseph. *Nebraska Wildlife Viewing Guide.* Helena, MT: Falcon Press, 1997.

Knue, Joseph. *North Dakota Wildlife Viewing Guide.* Helena, MT: Falcon Press, 1992.

Kress, Stephen W. *The Audubon Society Handbook for Birders.* New York: Charles Scribner's Sons, 1981.

McEneaney, Terry. *The Birder's Guide to Montana.* Helena, MT: Falcon Press, 1993.

Newberry, Todd, and Gene Holtan. *The Ardent Birder: On the Craft of Bird-watching.* Berkeley: Ten Speed Press, 2005.

Peterson, Richard A. *A Birdwatcher's Guide to the Black Hills and Adjacent Plains.* Vermillion, SD: PC Publishing, 1993.

South Dakota Ornithologists' Union. *The Birds of South Dakota,* 2nd Edition. Aberdeen, SD: 1991.

White, Mel. *National Geographic Guide to Birdwatching Sites: Western U.S.* Washington, D.C.: National Geographic Society, 1999.

Attracting Birds

Kress, Stephen W. *The Audubon Society Guide to Attracting Birds.* New York: Charles Scribner's Sons, 1985.

Mahnken, Jan. *Feeding the Birds.* Pownal, VT: Garden Way Publishing, 1989.

Bird Songs

Cornell University Laboratory of Ornithology. *A Field Guide to Western Bird Songs: Western North America.* Compact discs. New York: Cornell University, 1999.

Cornell University Laboratory of Ornithology. *A Field Guide to Western Bird Songs: Eastern and Central North America*. Compact discs. New York: Cornell University, 2002.

Walton, Richard K., Robert W. Lawson, and Roger Tory Peterson. *A Field Guide to Backyard Bird Song: Eastern and Central North America*. Compact discs. Houghton Mifflin Company, 1999.

———. *Birding by Ear: Eastern and Central North America*. Compact discs. Houghton Mifflin Company, 1999.

Periodicals and Organizations

North American Birds. Published 4 times a year by the American Birding Association. Contact American Birding Association. http://www.american birding.org/

Bird Watcher's Digest. Published 6 times a year. Contact *Bird Watcher's Digest*, P.O. Box 110, Marietta, OH 45750. http://www.birdwatchersdigest.com

Birder's World. Bimonthly publication for casual birdwatchers to serious birders; includes identification tips, photography pointers, advice for traveling birders, and more. http://www.birdersworld.com

Living Bird. Quarterly magazine of the Cornell Laboratory of Ornithology. Contact Cornell University Laboratory of Ornithology, 159 Sapsucker Woods Road, Ithaca, NY 14850. http://www.birds.cornell.edu

WildBird. Published monthly. Contact *WildBird* Magazine, P.O. Box 483, Mt. Morris, IL 61054-0483. http://www.animalnetwork.com/wildbird

Web Sites

General Web Sites

National Audubon Society http://www.audubon.org

National Geographic Society http://www.nationalgeographic.com

National Wildlife Federation http://www.nwf.org

National Wildlife Refuge System http://www.fws.gov/refuges/

Birding Pals http://www.birdingpal.org

Birding Web Sites

http://www.abcbirds.org

http://www.americanbirding.org

http://www.audubon.org

http://www.birding.about.com

http://www.birding.com

http://www.birdingpal.org

http://www.petersononline.com/birds/links/general.html

http://www.birds.cornell.edu

http://www.virtualbirder.com

http://www.wildbirds.com

http://www.wildlifephoto.net/index.html

BIRDING DESTINATIONS

Below are some recommended locations for birding in this region. Many of these locations have visitor centers that may be able to direct you to particular sites.

Most addresses listed are mailing addresses. Only general locations are given. Please check for the actual location and driving directions before you visit.

COLORADO

Colorado State Parks
http://parks.state.co.us/

Barr Lake State Park
Rocky Mountain Bird Observatory
(off I-76 northeast of Denver)
13401 Picadilly Rd.
Brighton, CO 80603
(303) 659-6005

Jackson Lake State Park
(north of I-76 between Denver and Sterling)
26363 County Road 3
Orchard, CO 80649
(303) 645-2551

Chatfield State Park
11500 N. Roxborough Park Road
Littleton, CO 80125
(303) 791-7275

Other Sites
South Platte River Greenway
30-mile trail between Chatfield State Park and downtown Denver
(303) 698-1322

Tamarack Ranch State Wildlife Area
(off I-76 northeast of Sterling on Hwy. 55)
Colorado Division of Wildlife
(303) 474-2711
http://wildlife.state.co.us/

Fort Collins Greenbelt
City of Fort Collins
(303) 491-1661
www.ci.fort-collins.co.us/

Wheat Ridge Greenbelt
City of Wheat Ridge
(303) 205-7554

Pawnee National Grasslands *and* Pawnee Buttes
(off Hwy. 14 between Fort Collins and Sterling)
U.S. Forest Service
2150 Centre Ave., Bldg. E
Fort Collins, CO 80526
(970) 295-6600
http://www.fs.fed.us/r2/arnf/

Rocky Mountain Arsenal National Wildlife Refuge
(11 miles northeast of Denver off I-70)
U.S. Fish & Wildlife Service
Building 121
Commerce City, CO 80022
(303) 289-0232
http://www.fws.gov/rockymountainarsenal/

MONTANA

U.S. Fish & Wildlife Service
www.fws.gov

Benton Lake National Wildlife Refuge
(10 miles north of Great Falls)
922 Bootlegger Trail
Great Falls, MT 59404
(406) 727-7400

Bowdoin National Wildlife Refuge
(north-central MT, off Hwy. 2 between
Havre and Glasgow)
194 Bowdoin Auto Tour Rd.
Malta, MT 59538
(406) 654-2863

Charles M. Russell National
  Wildlife Refuge
(125 miles along the Missouri River from
the Fort Peck Dam west to Hwy. 191)
P.O. Box 110
Airport Road
Lewistown, MT 59457
(406) 538-8706

Medicine Lake National Wildlife Refuge
(extreme northeastern MT between the
Missouri River and the Canadian border)
223 North Shore Rd.
Medicine Lake, MT 59247
(406) 789-2305

Montana Department of Fish, Wildlife, and Parks
http://fwp.mt.gov/default.html

Freezeout Lake Wildlife
  Management Area
(40 miles west of Great Falls along Hwy. 89
between Fairfield and Choteau)
(406) 454-3441

Giant Springs State Park
(northeast of Great Falls on the
  Missouri River)
4600 Giant Springs Rd.
Great Falls, MT 59405
(406) 454-5840.

Makoshika State Park
(just east of Glendive off I-94)
Box 1242
Glendive, MT 59330
(406) 377-6256

Medicine Rocks State Park
(southeastern MT, off Hwy. 7 between
Baker and Ekalaka)
P.O. Box 1630
Miles City, MT 59301
(406) 234-0900

Missouri Headwaters State Park
(4 miles northeast of Three Forks, off Hwy.
205, then onto Hwy 286)
1400 S. 19th St.
Bozeman, MT 59715
(406) 994-4042

Other Sites
Pompey's Pillar National Monument
(25 miles east of Billings off I-94)
Interpretive Center: (406) 875-2400
Bureau of Land Management
Billings Field Office
5001 Southgate Drive
Billings, MT 59101
(406) 896-5013
www.mt.blm.gov

NEBRASKA

U.S. Fish and Wildlife Service
www.fws.gov

Crescent Lake National Wildlife Refuge
(in the panhandle east of Scottsbluff)
10630 Rd. 181
Ellsworth, NE 69340
(308) 762-4893

DeSoto National Wildlife Refuge
(25 miles north of Omaha across the Iowa
border off I-29)
1434 316th Lane
Missouri Valley, IA 51555
(712) 642-4121

Fort Niobrara-Valentine National
Wildlife Refuge Complex
(north-central NE at the junction of
Hwys. 83 and 20)
Hidden Timber Route
HC 14, Box 67
Valentine, NE 69201
(402) 376-3789
Rainwater Basin Wetland
Management District
(complex of wetlands along the Platte River
in south-central NE)
P.O. Box 1686
Kearney, NE 68848
Office: (308) 236-5015
http://rainwater.fws.gov/

Nebraska Game and Parks Commission

http://www.ngpc.state.ne.us/

Burchard Lake Wildlife
Management Area
(South of Lincoln and Omaha, 4 miles
northeast of Burchard)
(402) 471-5558

Chadron State Park
(Pine Ridge in northwest NE in the
panhandle)
15951 Hwy 385
Chadron, NE 69337-7353
(308) 432-6167

Fort Kearney State Historical Park
and
Fort Kearney State Recreation Area
(south-central NE in the Platte River valley)
1020 V Road
Kearney, NE 68847-9804
(308) 865-5305

Fort Robinson State Park
(northwest NE in the panhandle on
Hwy. 20)
P.O. Box 392
Crawford, NE 69339-0392
(308) 665-2900

Indian Cave State Park
(southeast of Omaha and Lincoln off
Hwy. 64E)
65296 720 Rd.
Shubert, NE 68437-9801
(402) 883-2575

Platte River State Park
(between Ohama and Lincoln south of
I-80)
14421 346th St.
Louisville, NE 68037-3001
(402) 234-2217

Wildcat Hills State Recreation Area
and Nature Center
(south of Scottsbluff in the western
panhandle)
210615 Hwy. 71
Gering, NE 69341
(308) 436-3777

National Park Service

www.nps.gov

Agate Fossil Beds National Monument
(north of Scottsbluff in the
western panhandle)
301 River Road
Harrison, NE 69346-2734
(308) 668-2211

Scotts Bluff National Monument
(south of Scottsbluff in the
western panhandle)
190276 Hwy. 92 West
Gering, NE 69341-0027
(308) 436-4340

Other Sites

Fontenelle Forest Nature Center
1111 N. Bellevue Blvd., Bellevue
and
Neale Woods Nature Center
14323 Edith Marie Ave., Omaha
(402) 731-3140
http://www.fontenelleforest.org/

Crane Meadows Nature Center *and*
Nebraska Bird Observatory
(south side of exit 305 off I-80)
P.O. Box 90
Alda, NE 68810
308-382-1820
www.cranemeadows.org

Pioneers Park Nature Center
S. Coddington Ave. & W. Calvert St.
City of Lincoln Parks and Recreation
Lincoln, NE
(402) 441-7895

NORTH DAKOTA
U.S. Fish and Wildlife Service
http://mountain-prairie.fws.gov/

Arrowwood National Wildlife Refuge
(along the James River in east-central ND)
7745 11th St. SE
Pingree, North Dakota 58476-8308
(701) 285-3341

Chase Lake National Wildlife Refuge
(between Bismarck and Jamestown off I-94)
5924 19th St. SE
Woodworth, ND 58496
(701) 752-4218

Des Lacs National Wildlife Refuge
(along the Des Lacs River in northwestern
North Dakota)
Box 578
Kenmare, ND 58746
(701) 385-4046

J. Clark Salyer National Wildlife Refuge
(along the Souris River in north-central ND)
P. O. Box 66
Upham, ND 58789-0066
(701) 768-2548

Lake Ilo National Wildlife Refuge *and*
Audubon National Wildlife Refuge
(1 mile west of Dunn Center off State Hwy.
200 in west-central ND)
3275 11th St. NW
Coleharbor, ND 58531-9419
(701) 442-5474

Long Lake National Wildlife Refuge
(south-central ND southeast of Bismarck)
12000 353rd St. SE
Moffit, ND 58560-9704
(701) 387-4397

Lostwood National Wildlife Refuge
(northwestern ND)
8315 Hwy. 8
Kenmare, ND 58746-9046
(701) 848-2722

Tewaukon National Wildlife Refuge
(5 miles south of Cayuga on County
Road 12)
9754 143½ Ave. SE
Cayuga, ND 58013
(701) 724-3598

Upper Souris National Wildlife Refuge
(30 miles northwest of Minot)
17705 212th Ave. NW
Berthhold, ND 58718
(701) 468-5467

North Dakota State Parks
www.ndparks.com

Cross Ranch State Park
(along the Missouri River north of
Bismarck)
1403 River Rd.
Center, ND 58530
(701) 794-3731

Turtle River State Park
(22 miles west of Grand Forks on Hwy. 2)
3084 Park Ave.
Arvilla, ND 58214
(701) 594-4445

Other sites
Alkali Lake
(31 miles north of Williston off Hwy. 85 in
northwestern ND)
BLM
North Dakota Field Office
2933 Third Ave. W.
Dickinson, ND 58601-2619
(701) 227-7700

Sheyenne National Grassland
(southeastern ND)
U.S. Forest Service
P.O. Box 946
Lisbon, ND 58054
(701) 683-4342
www.fs.fed.us

Theodore Roosevelt National Park
(135 miles west of Bismarck
off I-94)
Box 7
Medora, ND 58645-0007
(701) 623-4466
www.nps.gov

SOUTH DAKOTA

Badlands National Park
(east of Rapid City in western SD)
25216 Ben Reifel Rd., P.O. Box 6
Interior, SD 57750
(605) 433-5361
www.nps.gov

Buffalo Gap National Grassland
(northeast of Badlands National Park off
I-90)
U.S. Forest Service
125 North Main Street
Chadron, NE 69337
(308) 432-0300
www.fs.fed.us

U.S. Fish and Wildlife Service
www.fws.gov

Karl E. Mundt National Wildlife Refuge
and
Lake Andes National Wildlife Refuge
(southeastern SD off Hwy. 18)
38672 291st Street
Lake Andes, SD 57356
(605) 487-7603

Lacreek National Wildlife Refuge
(south-central SD off Hwy. 18)
29746 Bird Rd.
Martin, SD 57551
(605) 685-6508

Sand Lake National Wildlife Refuge
(northeast SD, 27 miles northeast of
Aberdeen)
39650 Sand Lake Dr.
Columbia, SD 57433
(605) 885-6320

Waubay National Wildlife Refuge
44401 134A St.
Waubay, SD 57273
(605) 947-4521

South Dakota Game, Fish, and Parks
www.sdgfp.info

Bear Butte State Park
(6 miles northeast of Sturgis off SD
Hwy. 79)
Box 688 (E. Hwy. 79)
Sturgis, SD 57785
(605) 347-5240

Custer State Park
(south of Rapid City)
HC 83, Box 70
Custer, SD 57730
(605) 255-4515

Newton Hills State Park
(southeast of Sioux Falls, 6 miles south
of Canton off County 135)
28771 482nd Ave.
Canton, SD 57013
(605) 987-2263

Oakwood Lakes State Park
(7 miles north and 3 miles west of Volga, off
Hwy. 14. Or, use Exit 140 on I-29)
46109 202nd St.
Bruce, SD 57220
(605) 627-5441

WYOMING

Devils Tower National Monument
(northeast corner of WY)
P.O. Box 10
Devils Tower, WY 82714-0010
(307) 467-5283
www.nps.gov

Thunder Basin National Grassland
(northeastern WY between the Bighorn
Mountains and Black Hills—two parts)
2250 East Richards
Douglas, WY 82633
(307) 358-4690
www.fs.fed.us

SPECIES INDEX

ABOUT THE AUTHOR

Jan Wassink studied wildlife management at Colorado State University and Utah State University, and has photographed wildlife for over thirty years. He wrote and photographed *Birds of the Central Rockies*, *Mammals of the Central Rockies*, and *Birds of the Pacific Northwest Mountains*, published by Mountain Press, and *Idaho Wildlife*, in the American Geographic series. He currently writes a regular wildlife column for *Montana Living*. He has published numerous articles and photographs in a wide variety of publications.

Wassink lives in Kalispell, Montana, with his wife. They have three married sons.